KT-173-527

THE ILLUSTRATED ENCYCLOPEDIA OF
AQUARIUM FISH

The Illustrated Encyclopedia of

Aquarium Fish

By Stanislav Frank

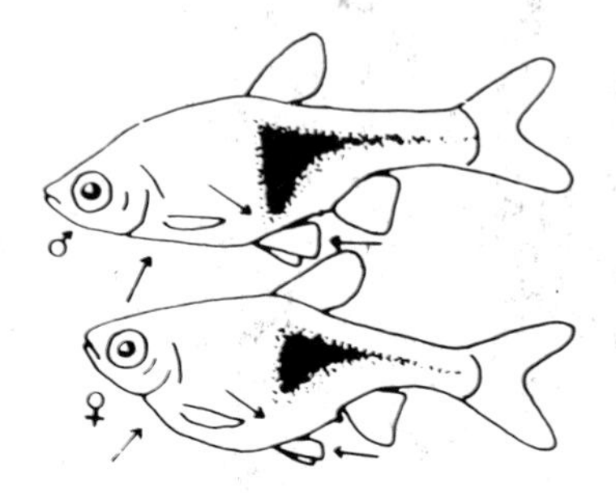

Frontispiece:
Spawning pair of Salmon-red Rainbowfish
(*Glossolepis incisus*); male above.

Page 5:
Male of the first filial generation of crossbreds of red
breeding veil form *Betta splendens* and *Betta imbellis*.

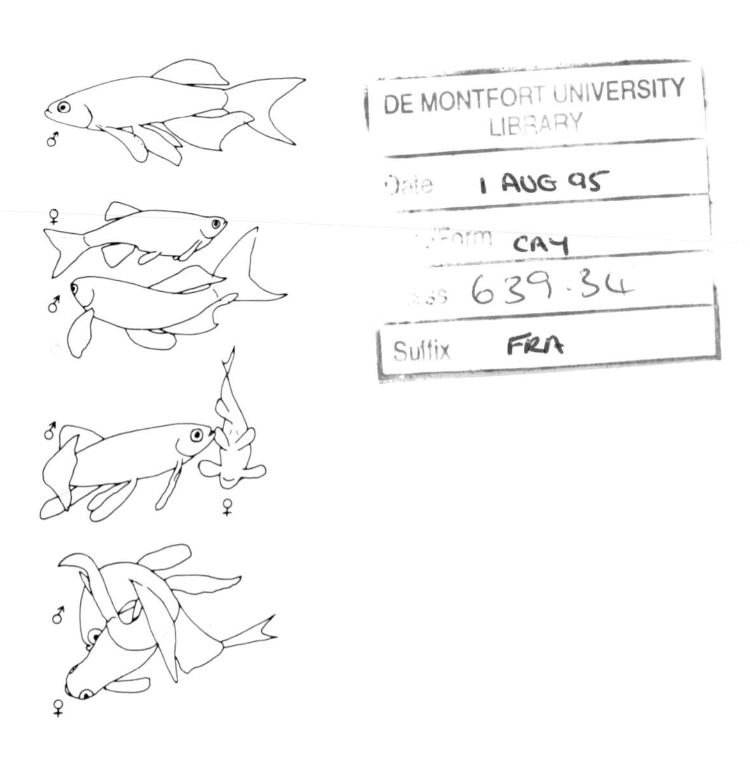

Text by Stanislav Frank
Translated by Edwin Kovanda
Photographs by Stanislav Frank et al.
Line drawings by Stanislav Frank
Graphic design by Karel Drchal

This edition published 1995
by Sunburst Books
Deacon House, 65 Old Church Street,
London SW3 5BS

ISBN 1 85778 086 8
Printed in the Czech Republic by Liberecké tiskárny, s.r.o., Liberec
3/23/01/51-01

CONTENTS

The World of Aquarium Fish in Colour 6
The Origin of Fish 6
Number of Species 7
Colouring 7
Chapter 1 Children of the Sun 9
2 Toothless but Still Mostly Carnivorous 49
3 The Knights of the Water Beds 83
4 Fishes Falling from the Sky 91
5 The Live-bearing Fishes 125
6 Monogamists with Refined Sense of Family Life 137
7 The Foamy Cradle for the Young 175
8 Curious Freshwater Fishes 193
9 Beauties of the Southern Seas 203
Bibliography 249
Index of Common Names 250
Index of Scientific Names 253

1

THE WORLD OF AQUARIUM FISH IN COLOUR

The word fish conjures up different images to different people. The sporting fisherman thinks of overpowering the largest catch, the scuba diver swims along intoxicated by mysterious underwater bushes and nooks of magnificent coral reefs, and the breeder of exotic fish is amazed at the display of colours and shapes of live fish in the aquarium. Many people, though deprived of such real experience, are nevertheless enticed and attracted to the silent underwater kingdom which is almost inaccessible to terrestrial creatures.

Fish have been an important part of man's diet, and in many parts of the world, especially in coastal regions, man lives almost exclusively on fish. Even in landlocked countries freshwater fish, inhabiting lakes and rivers, can be a considerable economic asset. Over the last one thousand years many ponds have been constructed for breeding fish for food or sport and there is a long history of nations keeping fish to please the human eye. China, for example, has an ancient tradition of breeding goldfish.

Modern aquaristics originated in science laboratories during the mid-19th century and was soon taken up by amateur breeders. It is now a popular hobby all over the world and often goes beyond a pastime. Many aquarists become ichthyologists and taxonomists. They make interesting and stimulating ethological observations, carry out genetic experiments with cross-breeding fish and collect fish that live in the wild. Some pursue their hobby alone while others work in cooperation with zoological or ichthyological institutions.

The most suitable fish species for aquarium breeding are those from tropical or subtropical regions. The fish remain very active throughout the year, do not require a winter rest period and are not dependent on seasonal or climatic changes. While the cool waters of the polar and temperate regions are inhabited by relatively few species, tropical and subtropical areas provide a suitable habitat for many small, colourful and often bizarrely shaped species. It is with the tropical fish that this book is concerned. The book does not give a strict systematic survey. Instead, fish species are grouped into chapters on the basis of similarities of environment or behaviour. However, their evolutionary relationships are not completely ignored.

THE ORIGIN OF FISH

Fish are gill-breathing vertebrates which, with some exceptions, live permanently in water. They first appeared in the Silurian period (450 million to 430 million years ago) and by the Devonian and Carboniferous periods (420 million to 350 million years ago) were widespread and possibly, in terms of different species, the most numerous inhabitants of the planet. It is difficult to decipher the different evolutionary lines of living species as fossil evidence is poor. The Indian Ocean, which has the richest fish fauna, is often considered to be the centre of diversification. Palaeontological finds of ancient fossil fish in freshwater deposits, and geological theories concerning the formation of continents and oceans do not, however, support this theory. Fish could have originated in freshwater and only later colonised the sea. Most ichthyologists are inclined today to believe that living species are partly of marine and partly of freshwater origin.

NUMBER OF SPECIES

The latest carefully researched estimate of the number of species currently living was made in 1970 by the American ichthyologist, D. M. Cohen. He estimated that there are about 50 species of Agnatha (jawless fishes), 515 to 555 species of Chondrichthyes (cartilaginous fishes) and 19,135 to 20,980 species of Osteichthyes (bony fishes). About 100 new species of fish are discovered and described every year.

Within the approximate number of 20,000 fish species there are:

Primary freshwater fish – 33.1 %
Secondary freshwater fish – 8.1 %
Alternating freshwater and sea fish (diadromous) – 0.6 %
Sea fish living in coastal warm water – 39.9 %
Sea fish living in coastal cold water – 5.6 %
Sea fish living at the sea bottom (benthonic) – 6.4 %
Sea fish living far from the coast close to the water surface (epipelagic) – 1.3 %
Fish living at depths of more than 200 metres – about 5.0 %

Freshwater fish comprise about 41.2 % of all fish species. These inhabitants of streams, rivers and lakes are most exposed to the direct influence of man and it is highly significant that almost half of the living species are subject directly to considerable changes in the environment and are endangered by human activity.

COLOURING

The colours of fish vary from silver-grey or grey-blue to very bright and patterned, and from translucent or white to dark brown and deep black. Colouring can be a sexual trait as well as a specific one. The males are usually more colourful than the females and in many tropical fish the colours of the sexes differ so greatly that males and females have been described as separate species. In some species the males become brilliantly coloured only during the breeding period.

Colour and body shape sometimes have a protective function and enable a fish to blend with its environment. Some seahorses and pipefish combine colour with filament-like projections from their bodies and so resemble sea algae.

The colour of a fish rarely remains unchanged. The pigmented cells, or chromatophores, are connected with nerve endings and this enables the fish to quickly change its colour and patterns. Plaice are a fine example; they change their colour and pattern to match the colour and simulate the texture of the seabed. In this way they become so perfectly camouflaged that it is very difficult to distinguish them from their surroundings. Many fish, such as species of *Poecilobrycon* and *Latris*, also change colour at night. Brighter colours generally disappear with age, when the fish usually turn dark and become less conspicuous.

Chapter 1 CHILDREN OF THE SUN

Neon Tetra [2] (*Paracheirodon innesi*) stands out boldly in a shoal and on the dark bottom of a dimly lighted aquarium.

Freshwaters of the tropical and subtropical regions of Africa and Central and South America are, as a rule, inhabited by large populations of colourful fish of the suborder Characinoidei which fully deserve their name 'children of the sun'. They live in all waters of the rain forests, from torrents to rivers, and in savanna regions with shallow waters which are exposed to the sun. These fish are mostly very thermophilic and are subject to only small fluctuations of temperature (ranging mostly within 1 to 2°C) during the day and throughout the year. The optimum temperature for keeping them in captivity is about 25°C. The majority of them are lively, sociable and gregarious. For this reason they have become popular with aquarists throughout the world as valuable members of aquarium fish communities. Of the wide variety of families belonging to this suborder, only the representatives of the best known will be mentioned. These include the Characidae, Hemiodontidae, the hatchetfish (Gasteropelecidae), Alestidae, Lebiasinidae, Citharinidae, Serrasalmidae, and Characidiidae. A few characoids, such as some representatives of the family Serrasalmidae, are true predators; these include the vicious Black Piranha, or piraya, which is among the most feared freshwater fish of South America.

Long-finned Characin [3, 4] (*Brycinus longipinnis*)

The native waters of this fish are in tropical West Africa from Sierra Leone down to the river Congo. The males are larger than females and grow to 13 cm in length. Secondary sexual differences in the Long-finned Characin are pronounced and conspicuous. The male's body is markedly elongate; the dorsal fin rays are frayed, the abdominal fins thread-like and the anal fin is arched with a whitish edge. In the females each fin is much shorter and the anal fin margin is straight or slightly concave.

◄2

3

4

The Long-finned Characin spawns for several months at two- to six-day intervals in open waters near plants, stones, pieces of wood, or roots. Its eggs are 2.5 mm across. The incubation time is approximately six days and the temperature of the water should be 26–28°C. Immediately after hatching the fry start filling their swimbladders and their nutrition changes from endogenous to exogenous. At first the freshly hatched fish swim upwards at an angle of 30–40°. Their larval size is 7.2 mm. Only soft water (not exceeding 3° dGH of total hardness) is suitable for them in aquarium fish culture. It is advisable to encourage the development of these fish by adding five to six drops of ToruMin for every four to five litres of water. Freshly hatched nauplii of the brine shrimp (*Artemia salina*) are suitable for the first food. Adult individuals feed mainly on flying insects. This food is hard to substitute in the aquarium; the banana flies of the genus *Drosophila* can be used as a suitable replacement. At hatching time the water in the reservoir should be intensely aerated, since it is easier for the young fish to abandon the egg case in water with an abundant supply of oxygen.

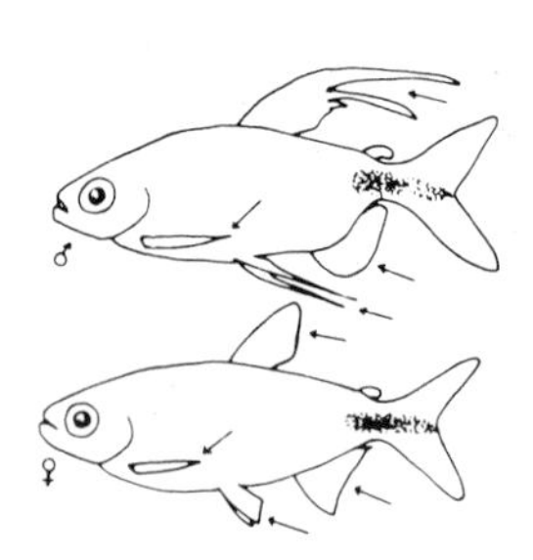

Brycinus longipinnis

Congo Tetra [5] (*Phenacogrammus interruptus*)

The Congo Tetra occurs only in the Congo basin in Africa. The males are larger than the females and grow to more than 12 cm long. The central rays of the caudal fin of the male [5, top] are elongate and form a lobe which is much longer than the fin itself. This beautiful characin varies in shape and colour. It spawns mostly in open waters on sunny days. The large eggs are light brown in colour and do not stick. When laid, they slowly fall to the bottom. The fry hatch at 26–27°C within six to seven days, and their further development is similar to that of the Long-finned Characin. The Congo Tetra is a very popular species, easy to keep, but it does not spawn easily.

5

Arnold's Red-eyed Characin [6] (*Arnoldichthys spilopterus*)

This fish is found in the tropical waters of West Africa. It has a spindle-shaped body about 7 cm in length. In this species the anal fin of the males [6] is convex while that of the females is concave. Breeding and rearing are the same as in the Long-finned Characin but the eggs are much smaller (about 1.2 mm across). Rolf Beck has observed that the embryos hatch very quickly (within 30–36 hours) and are underdeveloped. They begin to swim after seven days. At first the fry are very shy. They grow quickly and at the age of 14 days they are 15 mm long.

6

Black-line Tetra or **Scholze's Tetra** [7] (*Hyphessobrycon scholzei*)

The Pará basin in northern Brazil is the home of this fish. Adults are about 5 cm long. The male is slimmer than the female. This characin has no special requirements and reproduces readily at a temperature as low as 23°C. Their reproductive capacity is outstanding; up to 1,600 young fish can be obtained from one spawning. Large glass spawning reservoirs are needed to keep the water pure when rearing so many young. In aquaria they will eat dry, artificial or plant food as readily as live food.

7

8

Serpae Tetra [8] (*Hyphessobrycon serpae*)

The Serpae Tetra inhabits the Amazon and Río Guaporé basins. It grows to a length of about 5 cm. This species is closely related to the **Jewel Tetra** (*Hyphessobrycon callistus*) [9], from which it differs in the bright red, lighter and more pronounced colour of the body and fins, and in a spot behind the gill-covers. This mark is normally small and square and may be missing in some bright red aquarium populations of the species. In *Hyphessobrycon callistus* the mark is wedge-shaped. The Serpae Tetra is easy to keep and rear and needs practically the same treatment as *Hyphessobrycon ornatus*, which is described below. The only difference is the short life span of the Serpae Tetra, which rarely lives longer than two years in captivity. It often suffers from infectious dropsy, which is practically impossible to treat and soon kills the fish. Young Serpae Tetra readily reproduce throughout the year. They spawn over or near fine-leaved plants.

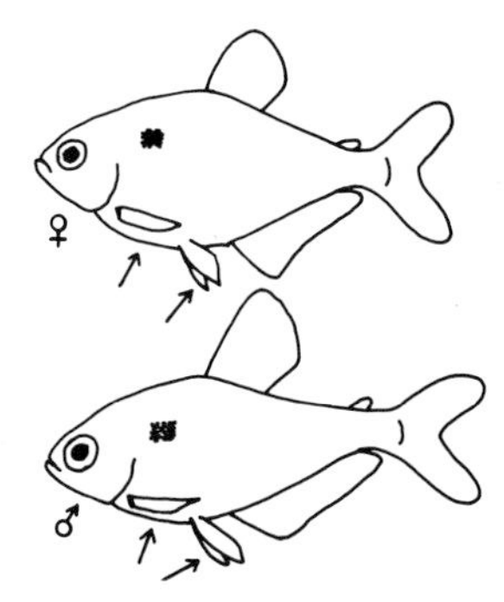

Hyphessobrycon serpae

Pink Jewelled Tetra [10] (*Hyphessobrycon ornatus*)

This fish, which comes from the lower reaches of the Amazon and from the rivers of Guyana, grows to 4–6 cm long. The sturdy characin is a good fish for common tanks. Excessively soft water is not recommended for keeping this species; it prefers water with a low carbonate content since the embryos are very sensitive to the presence of carbonates. Non-carbonate hardness should be no higher than 6° dNCH and the optimum pH should range about the neutral value. In water without hardness or in excessively acid water, many embryos suffer from constitutional dropsy; they fail to fill the swimbladder properly and do not start swimming. *Hyphessobrycon ornatus* is a very productive species, often giving five to six hundred young from one spawning. Advanced fry are fairly voracious and readily eat and quickly grow on the nauplii of brine shrimps. To avoid death of the young during the first three weeks, make certain the temperature does not drop below 27°C. The young fish are highly sensitive to increased nitrite content in the water. It is therefore necessary to remove the detritus regularly from the bottom and to add fresh water of the required temperature. Losses can also be avoided by timely transfer of the young fish to a swimming reservoir (a long, low and large container) with intensive aeration.

Sometimes the parent pairs refuse to spawn, or the first spawning yields just a few fertilized eggs. Such parents should not be replaced immediately but should be introduced again into the spawning aquarium after 14–17 days. Only the second spawning will show whether the two fish are fertile or not. Successful second spawning indicates that the initial failure was due to the over-ripened eggs of the female and that the two fish can make a good breeding pair. However, sometimes the male may be infertile and in this case must be replaced. The male initiates spawning by luring the female over a cluster of plants (such as *Fontinalis* and *Vesicularia*); then he presses closely to her

9

10

11

side, and after an abrupt jerk a small cloud of slightly sticky brownish eggs falls slowly to the bottom. The fry hatch at 27°C within 24–36 hours and start swimming after about five days. They will hide in plants for two or three weeks until they overcome their natural shyness. Then a small shoal of young fish appears in open water.

Lemon Tetra [11] (*Hyphessobrycon pulchripinnis*)

Though this fish also comes from Latin America, nothing certain is known about how widespread it is. In captivity it grows to a length of about 5 cm. The male is more robust, but slimmer, and the yellow-black colour of his fins is more pronounced. This beautiful, placid and popular characin has similar aquarium requirements to *Hyphessobrycon ornatus*. The only difference is that the Lemon Tetra is less sensitive to lower temperatures. The fry tolerate fluctuations between 24 and 26°C without problems.

Peruvian Tetra [12] (*Hyphessobrycon peruvianus*)

A native of the upper reaches of the rivers of the Amazon basin in Peru, in the neighbourhood of Iquitos, this small, finely coloured fish is no longer than 4 cm when adult. It is much sought after by aquarists but unfortunately only individual specimens are imported, usually together with other species which are offered in large lots. All attempts to reproduce it in captivity have so far been unsuccessful.

12

13

Flame Tetra or **Red Tetra** or **Tetra from Rio** [13, 14] (*Hyphessobrycon flammeus*)

This fish inhabits freshwaters near Rio de Janeiro. In aquariums it requires no special treatment. It is hardy and lively, and prefers the middle layers of water. The male [14, below] is slimmer, with a blood-red body and fins and black edge along the anal fin. The body colours of the female are not so conspicuous. The Flame Tetra tolerates

14

winter temperatures as low as 16°C. It is an excellent component of mixed aquarium communities. The fish will spawn in glass containers with a loosely floating tuft of plants, or in larger framed aquariums with standard equipment and a sandy bottom. They spawn both in pairs [13] and in shoals in the proximity of fine-leaved plants such as *Myriophyllum* and *Fontinalis*. The fry hatch from translucent eggs at water temperatures from 20 to 24°C within 24–36 hours. They hang on plants and aquarium walls until they start swimming (about five days). Flame Tetra fry readily consume not only all kinds of live food of adequate size, but also artificial feeds. However, artificial feed must be moistened before use to make it fall to the bottom, because the young fish do not pick their food on the surface.

Griem's Tetra [15] (*Hyphessobrycon griemi*)

A close relative of the Flame Tetra and Yellow Tetra, it comes from the Brazilian state of Goiás. This lively, gregarious fish grows to 4 cm in length. When excited, it takes on a red colour. The breeding practices are the same as in the Flame Tetra, but the temperature should never drop below 20°C and for successful development of the eggs and fry, softer water is needed (up to 7° dGH) with a pH of 7.

15

Flag Tetra [16] (*Hyphessobrycon heterorhabdus*)

This nimble, gregarious, and peaceable fish from the lower reaches of the Amazon and Río Tocantins grows to a length of 5 cm. The breeding and rearing requirements of this species in captivity are similar to those of the Flame Tetra. The Flag Tetra tolerates temperatures as low as 20°C. If the eggs and fry are to prosper they should be kept in slightly acid and very soft water (about 3° dNCH) with an admixture of peat extract. The optimum water temperature for spawning and rearing of the fry is 26°C. Young fish eat only live 'powder' food.

16

17

18

Tetra Perez or **Bleeding Heart Tetra** [17, 18] (*Hyphessobrycon erythrostigma*)

The *Hyphessobrycon erythrostigma* is better known to aquarists under invalid name *H. rubrostigma*. It comes from Colombia and grows to 10–12 cm long. This beautiful and decorative characin lives for a fairly long time. The male [18] is distinguished by its high, crescent-shaped dorsal fin. Information on the breeding of this species is scarce. The behaviour of the male in attracting the female [17] is similar to that of *H. ornatus*. Tetra Perez needs higher temperatures, at least 25–26°C, and varied food, particularly flying insects and larvae of chironomid midges, as well as artificial feeds such as 'TetraMin'. The imported specimens are usually severely infected with moulds. As they are very sensitive to any therapeutic chemicals, the treatment should be based on increased water temperature in the aquarium and frequent addition of fresh water. Fully mature males look stately when swimming around each other with their fins widely outstretched, a behaviour they often continue for several hours.

Head-and-tail-light Fish or **Beaconfish** [19] (*Hemigrammus ocellifer ocellifer*)

The native waters of this fish are in the Amazon basin and Guyana. It was imported to Europe as recently as 1960. Although it multiplied very quickly, it soon fell into oblivion again. Since 1910, aquarists have confused the Beaconfish and its subspecies, *H. ocellifer falsus*.

19

Pretty Tetra or **Garnet Tetra** [20] (*Hemigrammus pulcher*)

Inhabiting the Peruvian part of the Amazon near Iquitos, this is a quiet, gregarious fish about 5 cm long. For successful breeding a large glass tank (30–50 litres) is necessary because spawning is very vigorous. It is recommended to use only females with fully ripe eggs for spawning, otherwise the male may kill her in a short time. The pair of fish spawns in open waters, usually close to the surface. The parent fish take no care of the tiny, translucent eggs which sink to the bottom. The eggs prosper best in very soft water (rain, snow, or distilled water with a very small admixture of tapwater). The water should be slightly acid. The number of young ranges from 400 to 600.

20

21

Buenos Aires Tetra [21] (*Hemigrammus caudovittatus*)

This native of the Río de la Plata basin is about 10 cm long. Because it is easy to breed, it is recommended as a good species for beginners. The Buenos Aires Tetra tolerates temperatures down to 16°C. It is very voracious throughout its life. It feeds on common planktonic organisms (water fleas, *Cyclops*), inhabitants of the bottom (tubificid worms, larvae of chironomid midges) and artificial foods. It will bite aquarium plants and eat lettuce leaves, if offered. Neither the eggs nor the fry have any special requirements for water composition. They prosper in medium-hard tapwater.

Glow-light Tetra [22, 23] (*Hemigrammus erythrozonus*)

The Glow-light Tetra comes from Guyana and the female, which is larger than the male, grows to 4.5 cm long. A small all-glass tank with water hardness up to 8° dNCH will suffice for breeding. Although large quantities of fry will incubate in waters of low hard-

22

23

ness, most of the fry soon contract non-infectious, constitutional dropsy, and die within a short time. Carbonate hardness should not be higher than 1° dCH. The addition of a small amount of peat extract encourages the eggs to develop. Water temperature should be kept between 26 and 28°C. The breeding pair spawns in a thicket of fine-leaved plants [23] such as *Fontinalis* and *Vesicularia dubyana*. At the end of each spawning act, both fish turn upside down and the female ejects the eggs in this position. Sediment should always be removed and new water added during rearing in order to avoid an accumulation of nitrites which can be toxic to the fry. At first the young fishes are yellowish but later they develop a dark pattern all over the body. They consume relatively large pieces of live food such as nauplii of brine shrimp. They grow well and fast. In recent years a golden breeding form has become popular with aquarists.

Silver-tipped Tetra [24] (*Hasemania nana*)

This fish comes from the waters of south-east Brazil and grows to about 5 cm long. The female is yellow to olive green. The male is more slender and larger and is beautifully copper coloured. The body colouring of these fish varies a lot, depending on the origin and mood of the fish. The parent pair spawns in the evening under artificial light. When spawning, the fish squeeze their way through a dense tangle of aquatic plants. The eggs are small, about 1 mm across, very sticky and brown to black in colour. The fry hatch within 24–36 hours. The body of the young fish is translucent, but the yolk sac is opaque. After about three days they already have black eyes. They swim easily after five to six days. During this period they lose their shyness completely, swim freely about the glass tank and do not hide in the plants. At first they prefer rotifers and the *Cyclops* nauplii. They grow well.

24

25

Bleher's Tetra [25] (*Hemigrammus bleheri*)

This native of the Río Cuiuni, a tributary of the Río Negro, grows to about 4 cm in length. The imported fish, though shy at the beginning, soon get accustomed to life in captivity. The sexual differences are shown in colour picture 25 (male below, female above). For many years, this species was confused with the **Red** or **Rummy-nosed Tetra** (*H. rhodostomus*) and with the **Red-headed Tetra** (*Petitella georgiae*). Nowadays, however, this fish is very popular among aquarists; it is productive in the aquarium and noted for its attractive golden breeding form.

Red-headed Tetra [26] (*Petitella georgiae*)

The Río Huallaga in the upper reaches of the Peruvian Amazon and the neighbourhood of Iquitos to the east are the home of the Red-headed Tetra. The females are fairly big, some reaching a length of 6 cm. The males are smaller and more slender [26–two males]. The black crescent-shaped mark at the base of the tail is a conspicuous feature which distinguishes this fish from the Red-nosed Tetra and Bleher's Tetra. The colour of the tail fin is also different in the three above mentioned species. In *P. georgiae*, the red colour of the head extends only as far as the gill covers, whereas in the Bleher's Tetra it continues to form a wedge on the flanks, extending up to the dorsal fin [25]. For spawning in the aquarium, *Petitella* needs soft water kept at about 25°C. The fish are not very productive. The fry hatch within 30–36 hours.

26

Neon Tetra [27, 28, 29] (*Paracheirodon innesi*)

Living in the upper reaches of the Amazon and Río Purus, it grows to a length of 4 cm. The female is bigger than the male. For years the Neon Tetra belonged among the 'problematic fishes'. Only after World War II did aquarists discover the requirements for breeding. The water must be very soft, 1–2° dNCH (without carbonate hardness), and the pH should range between 6.2 and 6.8. A small admixture of peat extract is essential. The spawning temperature should be kept at 23 to 24°C. The breeding pair spawn over plants [28] and must be removed from the tank immediately after spawning, otherwise they will eat the eggs. The fry hatch after about 24 hours and learn to swim five days later. One spawning yields 70–250 young. After 14 days the young take on a red colour and the green-blue glittering stripe on their body appears at the age of 18–21 days. Except

27

28

during the spawning period, the breeding fish should be kept in colder water at temperatures lower than 20°C. At temperatures above 24°C the eggs quickly ripen in the females and spontaneously leave the body cavity without being fertilized. Females kept at above 24°C are not willing to spawn; their ventral line is straight, they resemble the males, seek fights, and are often unable to reproduce. Recently the golden aquarium mutant has been bred [27].

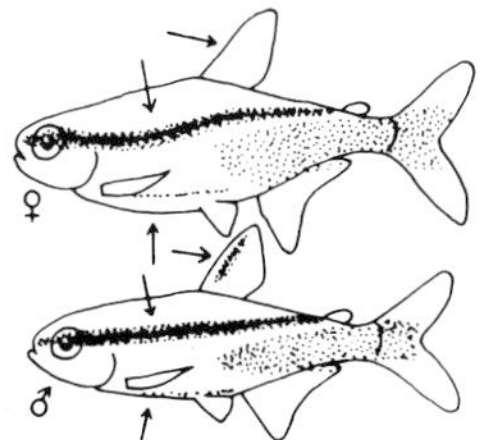

Paracheirodon innesi

29

Cardinal Tetra [30] (*Cheirodon axelrodi*)

It inhabits the southern tributaries of the Río Negro and the basin of the Orinoco. Fish imported from different localities differ in size and often in fin coloration. The females are bigger than the males and grow to a length of 5 cm. When their eggs are ripe, the female's belly is so deformed that she looks as if she is suffering from dropsy (see drawing). They spawn in open water at twilight and sometimes at night, or under weak artificial light. The eggs develop properly in soft water (about 1° dNCH) at a low pH value (5 to 5.5) without the addition of peat extract. At water temperature of 27 to 28°C the fry hatch within 18–20 hours. The young spend the next four days lying on the bottom and on the fifth or sixth day they fill their swimbladders and start swimming. They are very shy and sensitive to vibrations and abrupt changes of light. The Cardinal Tetra is highly fertile and 400 to 600 eggs from one female in one spawning are not exceptional. The fry grow very slowly. For five to six weeks they must be given live 'powder' food, rotifers, nauplii of *Cyclops* or brine shrimps, and should be fed a little several times a day. At the age of five weeks the fry are green coloured (longitudinal stripe) and their size is similar to that of the Neon Tetra when 17 days old.

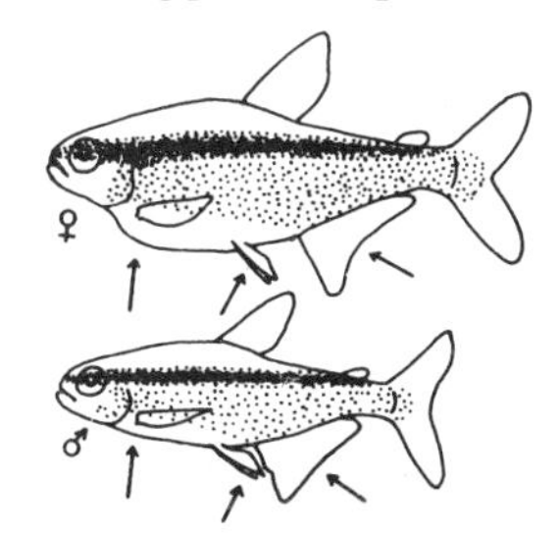

Cheirodon axelrodi

Other South American representatives of *Cheirodon*, such as *C. piaba*, *C. meinkeni* and *C. leuciscus*, have occasionally been imported. Only some of these have been successfully reproduced in captivity.

30

Blind Cave-fish [31] (*Anoptichthys jordani*)

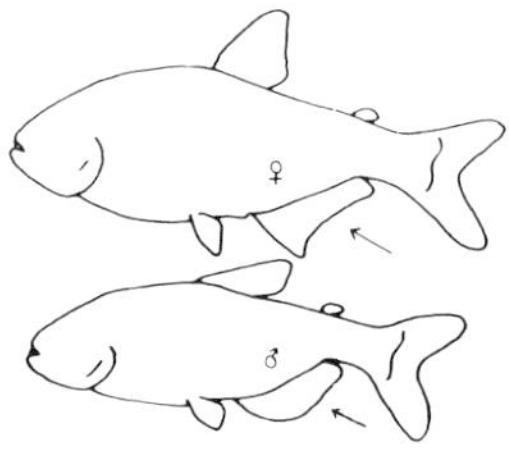

Anoptichthys jordani

This fish is abundant in the underground waters of the limestone caves (Cueva Chica) in the province of San Luis Potosí, Mexico. It is closely related to the surface-water subspecies *Astyanax fasciatus mexicanus* with which it can be successfully crossed to produce of fertile hybrids. This is why some ichthyologists do not treat it as a separate species, claiming that it is just a cave form of *A. f. mexicanus*. When kept under light in aquariums, the Blind Cave-fish changes its usual meat-red colour to silver. It grows to about 12 cm in length. The males are smaller than the females. The water should be hard (at least 15° dGH) and rather warm (26–27°C) to match water conditions in its natural environment. Fry emerge from the eggs with clearly visible black eyes. However, the eyes are not used for seeing, do not grow and steadily reduce in size. At fifty-two days the eyes become completely enclosed in a cartilaginous sheath which has developed from the white of the eye and it is covered with a thick layer of fat.

31

Bucktoothed Tetra [32] (*Exodon paradoxus*)

The *Exodon paradoxus* lives in the waters of the Río Branco, in northern Brazil, and the Rupununi, in Guyana. With its colourful appearance it would be a popular aquarium

32

species were it not for its highly predatory habits. The eggs are laid on plants and the fry hatch within 25–30 hours at 26–28°C. The species is difficult to breed and rear. It is only rarely imported.

Bloodfin [33] (*Aphyocharax anisitsi*)

Many other species of the genus *Aphyocharax* are imported from time to time, but they have never become permanently acclimatized in aquariums. The Bloodfin, a native of the Paraná in Argentina, is a lively and modest little fish which prefers sun-flooded aquariums. It grows to a length of about 5.5 cm. When spawning, it lays eggs on plants. The fry hatch at 24–28°C within about 30 hours. At first the young hang attached to the walls of the tank, to plants, or even to the water-surface membrane. After five days they will eat small live food as well as dry and artificial feed. The water in which the Bloodfin is kept must be crystalline-pure.

33

Red Phantom Tetra [34] (*Megalamphodus sweglesi*)

This fish lives in the Río Muco and in the upper part of the Río Meta in Colombia. It is about 4 cm in length. The water in which the fish is to be bred should be soft and slightly acid. The average number of young from one spawning ranges between 150 and 300. The fry grow very quickly. A shoal of orange-coloured fish in the green of an aquarium looks very conspicuous and attractive. The Red Phantom Tetra does not live long and often suffers from dropsy and plistophorosis. Another popular aquarium species is its close relative, the **Black Phantom Tetra** (*Megalamphodus megalopterus*), from the Río Guaporé of Brazil/Bolivia. It is fascinating to watch two males in threat display. The male has larger fins than the female and the colour of the fins is also different; the pelvic fins and the adipose fin are red in the female and grey to black in the male. The fry of the Black Phantom Tetra grow very slowly. Both species need water of the same temperature (from 23 to 26°C).

34

Diamond Tetra [35] (*Moenkhausia pittieri*)

Coming from Venezuela, it grows to about 6 cm long. It is not difficult to breed and rear this species, although it demands water of high quality – about the same as for the Neon Tetra (*Paracheirodon innesi*). The adults need a lot of space, hence the tank must be large.

Swordtailed Characin [36] (*Stevardia riisei*)

It inhabits the waters of Trinidad and northern Venezuela. The males grow up to 7 cm long and are larger than the females; their gill cover protrudes into a spoon-shaped process with a 'mirror' at the end. This characin is undemanding but prospers

35

only in aquariums with abundant vegetation. The courtship displays of this fish are interesting since the eggs are fertilized internally. The female then lays the eggs in the absence of the male. The fry hatch within 20–36 hours, the incubation time depending on water temperature (25–28°C).

36

Weitzman's Tetra [37] (*Poecilocharax weitzmani*)

This tetra is a native of South America in the upper Silimoes basin and in the freshwaters of the common upper reaches of the Río Negro and Orinoco in Venezuela. It belongs to the family Crenuchidae. The male is larger than the female; however, his length does not exceed 3 cm when adult. In the aquarium Weitzman's Tetra is very shy and likes semi-darkness and hiding places. It does not tolerate association with other fish species and consumes small live food of all kinds. The adult pair spawns inside vertical bamboo or vinidur tubes, about 20 cm long. The male treats the eggs and the fry hatched. When the young start swimming, their breeding and feeding on rotifers and the *Cyclops* nauplii are of no problem. Nevertheless, this characin requires frequent care and attention.

37

Penguin Fish [38] (*Thayeria obliqua*)

Inhabiting the Río Guaporé, which forms part of the Brazil/Bolivia frontier, it grows to a length of 8 cm. The species *T. sanctaemariae*, which is described later, and *T. obliqua* should be considered as the same species. The Penguin Fish is a lively and decorative fish, but unfortunately aquarists are entirely dependent on imports from its natural habitat since it has not yet reproduced in captivity. It is omnivorous but prefers planktonic food. It has often been confused with the following species.

Thayeria boehlkei [39]

The upper courses of the Marañón, a Peruvian tributary of the Amazon, are the home of this species, which grows to a length of 6 cm. Its lateral dark band extends from the hind edge of the gill cover. The body colour is the same in both sexes. The female looks

38

fuller in the pelvic region during the spawning period. There is also a difference in the shape of the swimbladder. Adult fish can be kept only in a well-covered aquarium since they are good jumpers. When fished with a net, imported individuals may jump a distance of two metres. For breeding this species, larger spawning tanks must be used with 30–40 litres of soft water at 3–5° dNCH and zero carbonate hardness. The optimal breeding temperature is 26°C. Aquatic plants are not necessary for breeding. The fish spawn in the evening under dim light and the spawning looks violent. The pH of the water should be kept above 7.0 throughout the development of the embryos and after hatching. Only live 'powder' food should be given to the swimming fry. The young fish grow quickly. When four weeks old, the fish is 10–12 mm long. A thousand young from one spawning is not exceptional.

39

Rachow's Pyrrhulina or **Fanning Characin** [40] (*Pyrrhulina rachoviana*)

A native of the lower reaches of the Paraná and La Plata in Argentina/Paraguay, it grows to 5–7 cm. The sexes differ only in the shape of the belly, which is more convex in the female [40, below]. It spawns readily on the leaves of plants or in small pits in sand.

40

41

Three-Banded Neolebias [41] (*Neolebias trilineatus*)

It inhabits the shallow waters of the upper Congo. The female is larger and grows to 4 cm long. This fish has been known in Europe for some time under the commercial name 'Goldneon'. It spawns in soft water in a thicket of plants. The fry are very shy. The fish have beautiful colours but their productivity is low.

Dwarf Pencilfish [42] (*Nannostomus marginatus*)

Native to the waters of Surinam and western Guyana, the Dwarf Pencilfish is a 4 cm long lively aquarium fish; its productivity is, however, low. Very small, three-litre glass aquariums will suffice for successful breeding of this fish. The water should be soft, up to 2° dNCH. The eggs are laid on plants and are sticky for a short time after being laid. Then they sink to the bottom. A yield of fifty to seventy young from one spawning can be regarded as a success. Soon after contact with the water the egg membrane swells up and creates a large translucent sphere around the egg. At 26°C the fry hatch within 30 hours. They are resistant to temperatures as low as 20°C. The just-hatched free eleutherembryos are nourished on endogenous nutrients from the yolk sac, and later the free swimming fry can eat large pieces of food such as nauplii of *Cyclops* and brine shrimp.

42

43

Three-banded Pencilfish [43, 44] (*Nannostomus trifasciatus*)

It is widely distributed in the basin of the middle reaches of the Amazon, in western Guyana and in the Río Negro. The females are larger than the males and grow to about 6 cm long. The spawning habits of the Three-banded Pencilfish are similar to those of the Dwarf Pencilfish. When preparing for spawning, the male makes typical swaying movements, bending the caudal peduncle downwards and letting it flex up again (see drawing A). He then approaches the female from the side and swims towards plants as if showing her the way. This play may last for varying lengths of time. Females with undeveloped eggs take on their nocturnal colours [44, above] and try to escape from the male by hiding in thickets of plants. Females with ripe eggs are normally longitudinally striped [44, bottom] and follow the male, letting him lead the way. The male immediately returns to the female, stops with his neck above the top of her head (see drawing B) and leads her gently towards the spawning substrate. This stage of courtship behaviour resembles the

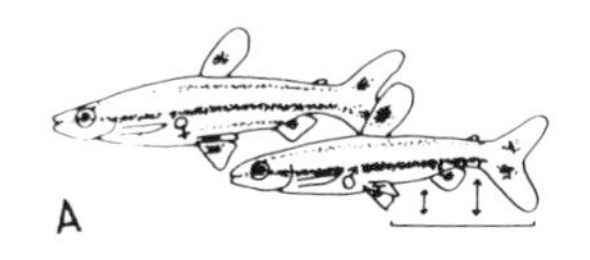

A – Nannostomus trifasciatus: the beginning of spawning – the male luring the female

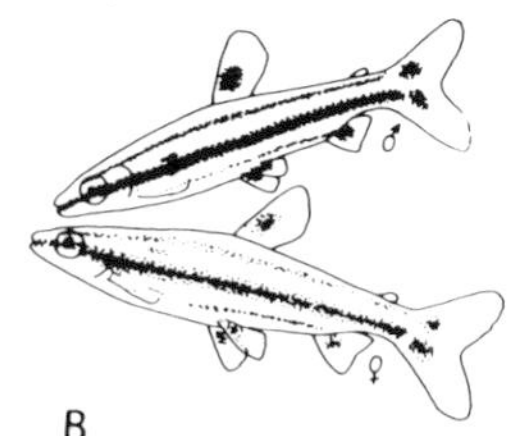

B – Nannostomus trifasciatus: just before spawning – the male guiding the female

44

courtship displays of the Tube-Mouthed Pencilfish (*Poecilobrycon eques*). The Three-banded Pencilfish lays the eggs on both broad-leaved and fine-leaved plants. The optimal water hardness for the proper development of the embryos is between 3 and 7° dNCH, pH of 6.6 to 6.8 and temperatures of 27 to 28°C. The eggs are comparatively large and are about 1.5 mm in diameter. The embryos develop for 24 hours inside the egg case. The species is difficult to breed and rear.

Espe's Pencilfish or **Barred Pencilfish** [45] (*Nannostomus espei*)

This species was described as recently as 1956. It is a native of the Río Mazaruni in Guyana and grows to a length of just 3.5 cm. The sexes can easily be distinguished by the shape of the caudal fin, which is long and spoon-shaped in the male. The spawning

45

act lasts half a minute to a minute. Rearing in captivity is successful only in exceptional cases. The young grow extraordinarily slowly and are very sensitive even to the smallest changes in chemical conditions of water.

Ansorge's African Pencilfish [46] (*Nannocharax ansorgei*)

Living in slow-moving waters of Nigeria, it grows to 4–5 cm. The differences between the sexes are not known. In captivity it prospers in shaded tanks. It is the only representative of the genus *Nannocharax* which prefers plankton food. The other species of the genus feed on the fauna of the substrate (Tubificidae, Chironomidae).

46

Tail-eye Pencilfish [47] (*Poecilobrycon unifasciatus ocellatus*)

This magnificent and elegant characin was first imported in 1949 from the Amazon basin and freshwaters of Guyana. It moves quietly but often fights with individuals of the same species. The Tail-eye Pencilfish has been bred occasionally in captivity but no details are available of its breeding requirements and it has not yet become popular among aquarists.

47

Tube-mouthed Pencilfish [48, 49] (*Poecilobrycon eques*)

This pencilfish lives in the basin of the middle reaches of the Amazon and in the Río Negro, where it keeps close to the banks near water plants and decaying wood. It grows to about 6 cm long. In captivity it prospers best when kept by itself. The fish will never show the full beauty of their colours in the presence of other species. They always swim at angle of about 45°. A ten-litre, all-glass tank will suffice for spawning. The water should be soft, up to 6° dNCH, and the pH should be about neutral (6.5–7.5). Breeding is often

48

successful in old aquarium water but water purity is the main requirement. The male is slimmer than the female and its pelvic fins have white margins and white tips.

Any broad-leaved plant will suffice for spawning. At each spawning act the female ejects 1–2 eggs and sticks them carefully to the underside of leaves. One spawning may yield up to 200 young. The temperature of the water should range between 22 and 28°C. At a temperature of 25°C the fry hatch within 24–36 hours and in 5–6 days start swimming after one another. They need exclusively live food when very young. Sexual maturity is reached within eight to ten months. In aquariums, the fish always keep in a shoal. The day colouring is shown in picture 48, the night colours in picture 49.

49

Marbled Hatchetfish [50] (*Carnegiella strigata*)

This fish inhabits the forest brooks of the Amazon basin and various waters in Guyana. It does not grow longer than 4.5 cm. In aquariums it is very voracious and feeds on insects like all hatchetfish. It can be given small insects of any species, which may either be caught in the wild or artificially bred at home, such as fruit or vinegar flies, 'banana flies', small cockroaches, crickets and larvae of gnats and chironomid midges. These should be dried in advance and floated on the water surface.

Hatchetfish need space to swim about. They belong to that category of fish which do not just glide but really fly. They move their pectoral fins quickly, swim some distance near the surface and, after breaking water, fly up to 3–5 metres over the water – a considerable accomplishment considering their small size. Their pectoral muscles are strongly developed.

50

51

Common Hatchetfish [51] (*Gasteropelecus sternicla*)

Coming from the Peruvian part of the Amazon basin, and from Guyana and Venezuela, it is larger than the Marbled Hatchetfish and grows up to 6.5 cm in length. In contrast to the Marbled Hatchetfish, it has a well-developed adipose fin. Hatchetfishes live in nature in shoals. When attacked by a predator, individual specimens swim rapidly in all directions, some jumping out of the water and 'flying' above the surface in an attempt to evade their pursuer. In the aquarium the fish requires a water temperature of 23 to 30°C; it can be reared with smaller peaceable fish species, staying in lower layers and near the bottom. No marked secondary sexual differences are known. In these transparent fishes the female is best distinguished, in a side view against light, by its eggs deposited in the ovary in its body cavity. Hatchetfish of the genera *Carnegiella* and *Gasteropelecus* reproduce in captivity. After the male's elaborate and energetic courtship, both partners remain close together, motionless in the water, close to plants, where they secrete eggs and milt. The fry hatch after some 30 hours.

52

The golden veil fins variety of **Rosy Barb** [52] (*Barbus conchonius*) is evidence of the fluctuating heredity of the species and of the patience and breeding skill of aquarists.

Chapter 2

TOOTHLESS BUT STILL MOSTLY CARNIVOROUS

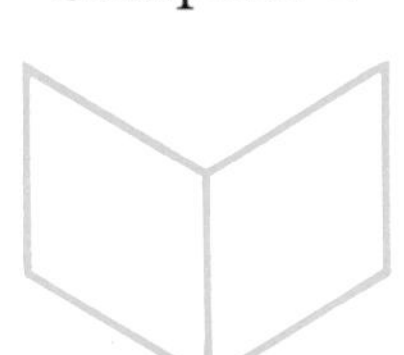

Toothless jaws are characteristic of the representatives of the large suborder of carps, Cyprinoidei. However, cyprinoids have one, two or three rows of well developed pharyngeal teeth carried on the altered fifth gill arch. Their distribution is almost world-wide: they are found in Europe, Asia, Africa, and North America and exclusively inhabit fresh waters. There are large differences in body shape between the individual species. About 1,500 species of this suborder are known and many of them are used for human consumption. Those of aquaristic interest are mostly the colourful tropical and subtropical species of the families Cyprinidae (carps), Cobitidae (loaches and spiny loaches) and Gyrinocheilidae. These fish are mainly placid and undemanding. They feed on zooplankton or seek their animal food with their tactile barbels on the bottom. Some species are herbivorous.

Goldfish [53] (*Carassius auratus auratus*)

The Goldfish comes from China, where the evidence regarding it goes back about one thousand years (to A.D. 970). In the 17th century it was introduced into Portugal and gradually it has spread through France and the Netherlands to the entire continent of Europe. Goldfish vary in shape and colour. The ground colouring is usually brass gold to red gold. White forms with red ventral part are known too, as are forms with a red dorsal body-part and black fins. The body is mostly covered with scales, but there are scaleless forms (mutants) as well. In the aquarium they are undemanding; they eat and feed on everything digestible: live animals, plants and artificial food. They are suitable for ornamental garden ponds and pools. In southern Europe and in warmer parts of the U.S. they can even overwinter in the open air. They are intensively bred in many coun-

53

tries; in France they are spawned out artificially. At first the young are of ordinary grey-green colour and they take on other colours as late as at 8 to 12 months of age. The huge variability of the Goldfish has been exploited for breeding forms of very bizarre shape and colour, designated as veiltail varieties.

Veiltail [54] (*Carassius auratus* var. *bicaudatus*)

This is a variety of the Goldfish (*Carassius auratus auratus*). Over a period of a thousand years, the Chinese have developed splendid varieties of Goldfish of many colours (grey, white, black, red and spotted) and many shapes (ovate without a dorsal fin) and some with eyes projecting strongly along the optic axis which are known as 'telescope veiltails', 'comets' and 'lionheads'. They are bred with the greatest care, but nevertheless only a small number of first-class individuals are found, since most of the progeny revert to the initial wild form in both shape and colours. Veiltail breeding is a constant test of patience.

54

55

Pearl Danio [55] (*Brachydanio albolineatus*)

This species from flowing waters of India and Sumatra grows to a length of 5.5 cm. The male is much slimmer than the female. Populations from different areas have different colours. The basic colours are green, shining gold, violet, and blue. Some of these colour variants have become common aquarium stocks. Breeding is simple. A small, 10-litre all-glass tank containing tapwater which has been left to stand for a few hours will suffice for spawning. Shallow water, no deeper than 10 cm, is preferred by the spawning fish. Water temperature should be 24–28°C. The Pearl Danio likes to spawn just beneath the surface of the water, over a thicket of water plants (such as *Fontinalis* and *Myriophyllum*). Spawning is vigorous. To ensure successful spawning two to three males per female should always be placed together in the breeding tank. If overripened eggs block the urino-genital pore the female then 'hardens' and is no longer capable of further spawning. The breeding fish should be removed after spawning to prevent them eating the eggs. The fry emerge from the eggs within three days (at a temperature of 26°C) and hang on to plants or the sides of the tank or lie on the bottom. They start swimming after 5–6 days.

Blue Danio [56] (*Brachydanio kerri*)

It comes from the Koh Yao and Koh Yao Noi islands in Thailand and grows to a length of about 4 cm. In the period of spawning its body is bluish and its fins are yellowish. It has a pair of short barbels on the upper jaw, while in each corner of the mouth it has one long barbel. The lateral line is missing. The breeding is identical to that of *B. albolineatus*.

56

Zebra Danio [57, 59] (*Brachydanio rerio*)

A native of the eastern part of India, it grows to a length of 4.5 cm. A temperature of about 24°C is sufficient for breeding this species in captivity. Some females are faithful

57

58

to their mates and readily spawn repeatedly with the same partner. In winter the Zebra Danio can be kept in unheated aquariums at temperatures as low as 16°C. The requirements are similar to those of the Pearl Danio. The breeding pair usually spawns near the tank bottom. Much admired by breeders is a veil-fin mutant [57] selected and bred in the aquarium, and the veil form of **Leopard Danio** (*Brachydanio frankei*) [58].

59

Spotted Danio [60] (*Brachydanio nigrofasciatus*)

The habitat of this fish, which grows to 4 cm, is in rivers and ponds of Burma. Very small all-glass tanks can be used for breeding it in captivity. The Spotted Danio is a warmth-loving species, spawning at 26–28°C at various water layers in thickets of fine-leaved plants. The breeding tanks should be deep. About 60 eggs are produced by one female but two-thirds of these eggs usually remain unfertilized. It is therefore suggested that spawning fish be placed in the breeding tank in shoals. It is also advisible to shade the tank to prevent the adults from eating the eggs which settle on the bottom. Alternatively a fine-mesh plastic grid may be placed under the water plants to save the eggs which have fallen to the bottom. The productivity of the Spotted Danio is low. The fry are reared like those of the Pearl Danio.

While the Zebra Danio (*Brachydanio rerio*) has two pairs of barbels, the Spotted Danio (*B. nigrofasciatus*) has only a single pair and colouring is markedly different too. The latter has an olive-brown dorsal body part, while the abdominal part is yellowish-white. Two blue-black bands run from the upper back part of the gill cover to the central rays of the caudal fin. The upper band is narrower, the lower wider, and there are numerous

60

blue spots beneath them. The dorsal, anal and caudal fins are yellow. Blue points form lengthwise lines in the anal fin, whose outer edge is yellow. The female's ventral fins are white-yellow, while the more slender male's are orange. To distinguish the sex of the fish is no problem. The male is below in the picture.

61

Giant Danio [61,62, 63] (*Danio aequipinnatus*)

The Giant Danio lives in clear flowing waters on the west coast of India and in Sri Lanka. In its natural habitat it grows to 15 cm long. In captivity specimens of only 6–7 cm in length are usually sexually mature. This lively fish spends most of its life near the water surface. The dominant individuals usually swim in the middle of the shoal. They have more pronounced colours and swim horizontally, whereas the weaker fish are paler and keep to the edges of the shoal, swimming in a somewhat slanted position. If the dominant individuals are removed their position is immediately taken by the next strongest fish. Rearing and breeding is similar to that of the Zebra Danio but because this species is larger the tanks should be bigger, with enough space

62

Danio aequipinnatus

for the fish to swim about. Spawning is vigorous. After each spawning act a cloud of eggs falls to the bottom. The fry are voracious from the very beginning and they feed on both live and artificial food. They can even be fed with substitute food such as a pap from hard-boiled egg yolk and a little water. They grow rapidly on sufficient food. Frequent cleaning of the tank and partial water replacement are recommended.

63

Fireglow Barb or **Ember Barb** [64] (*Barbus fasciatus*)

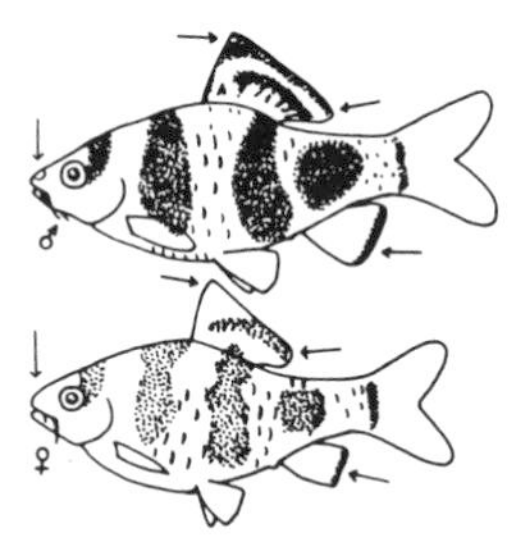

Barbus fasciatus

The native waters of this species are in south-eastern India and the islands of Sumatra and Borneo. Adult males are 10–12 cm long. The basic colour is wine red to violet, with irregularly distributed black blotches which vary in shape but merge to form five stripes. Three-week old fry have only three transverse stripes. This species is difficult to breed. The fish are notorious fighters and the male often kills the female. The eggs are very sticky (a plastic spawning grid cannot be used) and the parents are enthusiastic spawn-robbers. The requirements of this species for water composition are high. The eggs and fry

do well only in soft (2–3°dNCH), and chemically and biologically clean water. Advanced fry must be gradually acclimatized to harder water (this applies mainly to carbonate hardness). The adults, on the other hand, are tolerant of water composition and can live for many years in richly planted tanks.

65

Five-banded Barb [65] (*Barbus pentazona pentazona*)

Living in the waters of the Malay Peninsula, Singapore, south-eastern Borneo and Sumatra, it grows to about 5 cm long. At breeding time the females of this undemanding aquarium pet are much larger than at other times. Their basic colour is yellow to orange and the fins of the males are dark red. One female lays 300–400 large eggs at a time. The robust fry hatch at a water temperature of 26°C within 26–30 hours and begin to swim freely and hunt for live food after six days. Rearing is easy because the fry grow quickly from the beginning. However, the growth of the young is slowed down, or even arrested, at the age of 10–12 months. Commercial breeding of this fish is not profitable, since they do not command a high price and food consumption is high.

Barbus barilioides [66]

This fish comes from South Africa, Zambia and southern Zaïre. The female, which is larger than the male, grows up to 6 cm long. This small fish has an elongated body. It is shy in aquariums and usually stays near the bottom or in the middle layers of the tank. However, if not disturbed, it is lively and likes to swim about. It is tolerant of the presence of other fish and can be kept in all-glass tanks of at least 10 litre capacity. It can be given food of all kinds. The water should be soft, about 3° dGH. *Myriophyllum* or *Fontinalis* provide a good spawning substrate. The temperature of the water should range between 24 and 26°C with a pH of 7.0. One spawning may yield up to 250 eggs. The fry hatch at 25°C within 24 hours and start swimming freely after three days; they will take the nauplii of *Cyclops* from the beginning. After three weeks the young fish grow to 18–20 mm and have the first two thin transverse stripes on their sides. The sexes can be distinguished easily from the age of 4 months. The males remain smaller and very slender.

66

Spanner Barb [67] (*Barbus lateristriga*)

This lively shoaling fish from the waters of the Malay Peninsula, Singapore, and the Greater and Lesser Sunda Islands of Indonesia grows to a length of 20 cm. The female is much larger than the slimmer male. The dorsal fin of the male is deep red at the base. Despite its comparatively large size, this barb is elegant and peaceable. Its fertility is high. The breeding tank should be planted with robust water vegetation since the fish spend most of their time near the bottom, always chewing at something and digging continuously in the upper layers of the soil. Finer plants would be damaged by them.

67

68

Sumatra Barb or **Tiger Barb** [68, 69, 70] (*Barbus tetrazona*)

Native to the stagnant or slowly flowing freshwaters of Sumatra and south-eastern Borneo, it grows to about 7 cm long. The Sumatra Barb is a lively shoaling fish, which needs soft, well-filtered and crystalline-clean water. It cannot be kept with slow-swimming fish because it likes to nip the ends of their fins. The optimum water temperature is between 20 and 26°C. Larger tanks should be used for breeding, since in large aquariums the male does not pursue the female so vigorously. Lower temperatures, between 21 and 23°C, may also contribute to less vigorous spawning. The water should be no harder than 3–5° dNCH and carbonate hardness should be lower than 1° dCH. It is advisable to add a small amount of peat extract. Six to seven hundred eggs are produced at a spawning. The eggs are large and yellowish, and the fry hatch at an average temperature of 24°C within 36 hours. After five days the fry swim freely. They are robust and readily take 'powder' food. They grow quickly.

Various mutants have been bred from the original form in recent years. The main ones are the yellow (xanthoric) forms with black eyes, albinos with red eyes [69], red-bellied albinos called 'Hong-Kong', and moss green lustrous specimens with transverse bands fused into a uniform background with a green sheen on top. These mutant forms are delicate and prefer warmth.

69

70

Golden Barb or **Schubert's Barb** [71] (*Barbus 'schuberti'*)

This barb is unknown in the wild. Its morphological and anatomical characteristics are the same as those of the Chinese Barb, so it is undoubtedly a xanthoric mutation of *Barbus semifasciolatus.* There are various intermediate types, such as spotted, pure gold, or even albinotic red-eyed specimens, and strange albinos with black fins.

This is a delightful aquarium species which attractively shows its glittering gold colour against a green background of water plants. It is also appreciated for its activity and restlessness. The Golden Barb is smaller than the Chinese Barb. The females are larger than the males, but their length does not exceed 7 cm. It is omnivorous and warmth-loving. The temperature of the water should not drop below 20°C.

71

Stoliczka's Barb [72] (*Barbus stoliczkanus*)

Inhabiting the lower part of the basin of the Irrawaddy river in Burma, it grows to a length of about 6 cm and stands temperature changes between 18 and 25°C. The males are splendidly coloured. At water temperatures between 24 and 26°C the fry hatch within 24–30 hours. Rearing on live 'powder' food presents no problem. The adult fishes are docile and their colours are more pronounced in well planted and overgrown aquariums. They have few special requirements for water composition. The males often 'show off' the splendid colours of their dorsal fins.

73

Striped or **Zebra Barb** [73, 74, 75] (*Barbus lineatus*)

This species was imported from the Malay Peninsula. The female, which is larger than the male, grows to a length of 12 cm in the wild and to about 6 cm in aquariums. The body is elongate and the ground colour is yellowish silver; the sides are decorated by

74

75

four to six dark blue to blue-black longitudinal bands. In females the colouring is less pronounced. This species is not very widespread among aquarists, although it is fairly prolific and breeds easily. It is a suitable fish for community tanks, owing to its liveliness and tolerance of other species. It is highly susceptible to infectious dropsy, which may kill whole populations in excessively soft water or in old water with a high nitrite and nitrate content.

76

Black-spot Barb [76] (*Barbus filamentosus*)

The Black-spot Barb comes from the western part of southern India, where it grows to a length of 15 cm. In captivity it is usually smaller (up to 10 cm long). The males are smaller than the females and their dorsal fin rays are elongated. Breeding is simple in large aquariums. The fish often spawn in shoals. The young differ in colour from the adults; they have two wide black transverse bands on their flanks, another narrower band at the base of the tail, and still another, fainter line on the top of the head. The fins of the young are orange to brick red. In half-grown specimens the base of the tail is reddish with a red blotch in each lobe protruding into a white tip.

77

Aquarists often confuse this barbel-less fish with another species, *Barbus mahecola*, which has practically the same colours but differs from *B. filamentosus* by having two maxillary barbels at the corners of the mouth. The Black-spot Barb withstands water temperatures fluctuating between 17 and 25°C.

Odessa Barb [77] (*Barbus* sp.)

Its country of origin is unknown. It appeared on the fish market in Odessa (Ukraine) in 1971 and the next year it was introduced into Europe. This fish has been subjected to detailed study and was found to be a relative of the **Twospot Barb** (*Barbus ticto*). It reproduces readily in captivity. The males display the splendid red colour comparatively late, at about 10–12 months of age. The eggs and embryos need soft water (up to 7° dGH) at 25–26°C.

78

Black Ruby, **Nigger Barb** or **Purple-headed Barb** [78] (*Barbus nigrofasciatus*)

This fish comes from shallow, slow-flowing waters in southern Sri Lanka. The adults are about 6 cm long. It is suitable for beginners because it survives room temperatures of about 14–16°C in winter. Fish that have been kept at low temperatures in winter spawn very readily in spring at temperatures between 18 and 22°C and are very prolific. If kept permanently in heated tanks at temperatures from 20 to 28°C, they never show the full beauty of their colours and are reluctant to spawn. At spawning time the male takes on a splendid purple colour on the front part of his body and his head; his back is velvet black with a green sheen. This species likes to spawn in morning sunshine in a large, normally planted aquarium with sandy bottom soil. The composition of the water is not important. Adult specimens are omnivorous.

79

Harlequin Fish or **Red Rasbora** [79] (*Rasbora heteromorpha*)

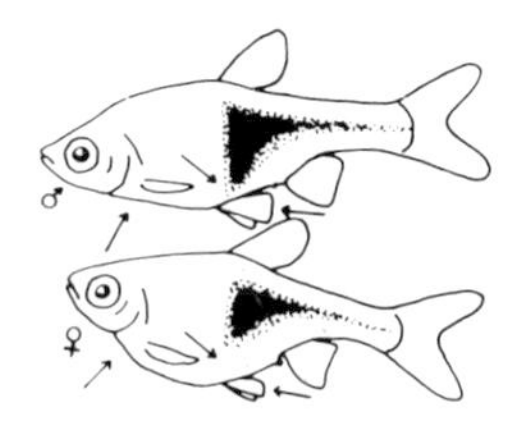
Rasbora heteromorpha

It is distributed throughout the Malay Peninsula, Thailand and eastern Sumatra. Adult specimens are no longer than 4.5 cm. In Europe it is one of the most popular shoaling fish kept in community tanks. The male is slimmer and the lower anterior corner of the dark wedge blotch extends up to the base of the pelvic fins (see drawing). An all-glass aquarium with 10 litres of water will suffice for spawning. The optimum water hardness is 3–5° dNCH and 0–1° dCH. If total hardness exceeds 6° the mortality of embryos rapidly increases during development. The natural mortality rate from egg fertilization to free swimming is about 10 per cent. A small amount of peat extract is recommended. Water temperature should be between 26 and 28°C and the pH neutral. During spawning both the male and female turn upside down and the female attaches the eggs to the underside of the larger and stronger leaves of water plants such as *Cryptocoryne* and *Ludwigia*. The parents do not care for the eggs. After spawning, the parent fish should be removed. The fry hatch from the large eggs after 24–28 hours and start swimming after five days.

80

Pearly Rasbora [80] (*Rasbora vaterifloris*)

The adults of this species from Sri Lanka are 4 cm long. The male is larger than the female and has stronger fins. The fish is splendidly coloured from pearly to rainbow. The breeding and rearing of the species is similar to that of the Harlequin Fish. The Pearly Rasbora prefers fine-leaved plants for spawning.

White Cloud Mountain Minnow [81] (*Tanichthys albonubes*)

This aquarium fish, particularly popular with beginners, comes from waters of the White Cloud Mountains near Quangzhou (Canton) and from waters near Hong Kong. It is about 4 cm long. Its colours vary greatly in the wild and in captivity. If it is gradually acclimatized, the White Cloud Mountain Minnow can survive winter temperatures as low as 5°C. Temperatures from 20 to 22°C are needed for spawning. The fish is omnivorous and lives in water of almost any composition. It spawns on plants in dense thickets of aquatic vegetation. The breeding pairs do not eat the eggs or the fry, so the young can be kept together with the parents. The fry hatch after 48–56 hours at 22–25°C and hang onto plants for three or four days; they then start swimming freely. At first they keep in a shoal just below the surface. They are best fed with dry and crushed food or the finest 'powder' food which they pick from the surface. After 10 days the fish can be given nauplii of *Cyclops* and brine shrimp. Gold-backed or veiled mutant specimens [81] are also kept in aquariums.

81

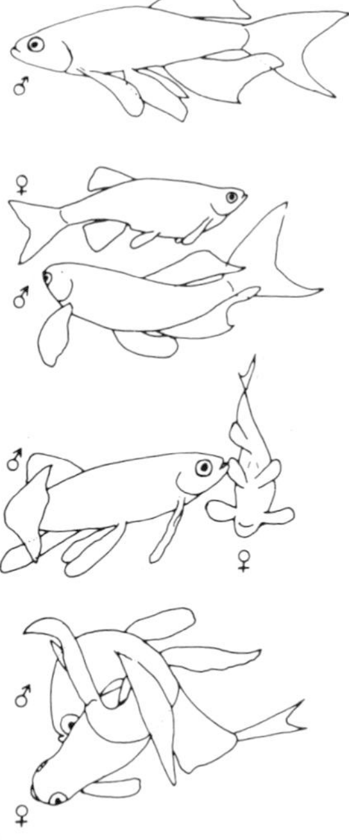

Secondary sexual difference in veil breeding form of *Tanichthys albonubes*. The male courts the female by spreading its fins and touching her sides with his mouth. Spawning act.

82

Flying Fox [82] (*Epalzeorhynchus kallopterus*)

This rare species is native to Sumatra and south-eastern Borneo. In the wild it grows to 14 cm in length; in captivity it is never longer than 10 cm. This species belongs to a subfamily, the Garrinae, which have a sucking mouth. Most representatives of this subfamily have torpedo-shaped bodies. The edges of the jaws are sharp and are adapted for grazing on algae and other vegetation. Many species are easy to keep in aquariums at water temperatures between 22 and 26°C. The Flying Fox needs a large tank and has no special requirements for water condition and vegetation. It soon removes the covering of algae from tank walls, cleans stones and plants within a short time and picks anything that is edible from the substrate. It will also eat animal foods of all kinds. When resting it lies on the bottom, on stones, roots or the broad leaves of plants. Although it prefers to live alone and drives all other fishes out of its territory, it does not harm them. In its islands of origin it is used as a food fish. Nothing is known about its breeding in captivity.

Siamese Flying Fox [83] (*Epalzeorhynchus siamensis*)

It comes from Thailand, from the upper basin of the Tadi river, and from the Malay Peninsula. Adults grow to 14 cm long. Aquarists can obtain only imported specimens since nothing is known about either sexual differences or breeding in captivity. Care in aquariums is the same as that described for the Flying Fox.

83

84

Bala 'Shark' [84] (*Balantiocheilus melanopterus*)

This fish lives in Thailand, south-eastern Borneo and Sumatra, where it inhabits water channels and flowing waters. In the wild it may grow up to 35 cm long. As Meinken pointed out, the female has a markedly larger belly than the male, even when just 15 cm long. Only the smaller, younger specimens are suitable for keeping in small aquariums. Adult specimens are good showpieces for public aquariums. The species is very hardy and is omnivorous. It is a good swimmer and a strong jumper. It constantly searches for food on the bottom, looking under stones or grubbing in the sand. Supplementary plant food is recommended from time to time, otherwise the fish may suffer nutritional defects. Nothing is known about its reproduction. Temperatures from 23 to 26°C seem to be optimal for this species. *Balantiocheilus melanopterus* sometimes produces short, sharp sounds. It prospers in the company of representatives of the closely related genus *Labeo*.

85

Red-tailed Black 'Shark' [85] (*Labeo bicolor*)

Living in brooks of Thailand, it grows to approximately 12 cm long. Its ventral mouth is provided with two pairs of barbels. The lips unite to form a sucking organ, which is provided internally with sharp ridges and horny tubercles. The male is more slender than the female. This fish prospers best in soft water which has been filtered through a thin layer of peat. Frequent additions of fresh water are recommended. Water temperature should range between 24 and 27°C. The tank must be shaded and richly planted so that the fish has hiding places under roots, stones, and so forth. Although the species is omnivorous, it likes to graze on coatings of algae and will also accept lettuce. Unfortunately, these fish often quarrel among themselves and should therefore be kept in large tanks. The dominant individual defends a large territory, which is often the whole tank, and brutally drives away the weaker fish. Violent fights can be prevented by reducing the water temperature to 21°C, but this temperature cannot be borne for long by the weaker individuals. Spawning in captivity has been observed several times but never described in detail.

Bridle 'Shark' [86] (*Labeo frenatus*)

This species from northern Thailand grows to approximately 8 cm long. Its ground colour is grey-green to brown-green and the belly is bronze to white. The anal fin of the male reportedly has a black edge. These fish are very useful in aquariums, where they eat any algal coating. They are much less quarrelsome than *L. bicolor*, but share some of its shyness and like to hide in flower pots or cut-up coconut shells.

The fish spawns in fast-flowing water in the aquarium. A single pair produces 2,000 to 4,000 eggs from each spawning; they are about 3 mm in diameter after fertilization and swelling. The fry are robust and will eat *Artemia* nauplii immediately they begin swimming. Rearing these fish is simple; they must have pure, well-oxygenated, continuously circulated water.

The genus *Morulius* is closely related to the genus *Labeo*. The **Black 'Shark'** (*Morulius chrysophekadion*), which has a strongly developed dorsal fin, is kept most frequently in aquariums. It comes from Thailand and the Greater Sunda Islands of Indonesia, where it grows to 60 cm long. It grows quickly in captivity and is very voracious; it constantly seeks food on the bottom and is partial to any kind of food. The Black Shark makes a lovely exhibit for large aquariums.

86

Chinese Algae-eater [87, 88] (*Gyrinocheilus kaznakovi*)

This is a native of Thailand. The length of the adults is about 30 cm. It belongs to the family Gyrinocheilidae, which is closely related to carps and carp-like fish. This family has only one genus; to date, three species have been described. They have no pharyngeal teeth. Apart from the usual gill-opening there is an additional aperture. The fish may remain attached to the ground for a long time without losing their respirating ability. They take the water in through a special aperture at the upper edge of the gill cover and discharge it under the lower edge (see drawing). The larger the fish, the finer their colours.

The *Gyrinocheilus kaznakovi* has a ventral mouth with well-developed lips which together form a sucker. The lips are provided with rasp-like folds for scraping the algae from the substrate. The fish is a stream-dweller and mainly inhabits brooks. In aquariums it is one of the best algae eaters, removing the algal cover from the leaves of plants and from tank equipment. It is not entirely dependent on algal food. Animal food, e.g. *Tubifex*-worms, dried and artificial food and dead plankton which has fallen to the bottom is also greedily eaten. The fish are very voracious. Larger specimens are often dangerous to other inhabitants of the tank. They can fasten on to other fish, damaging

87

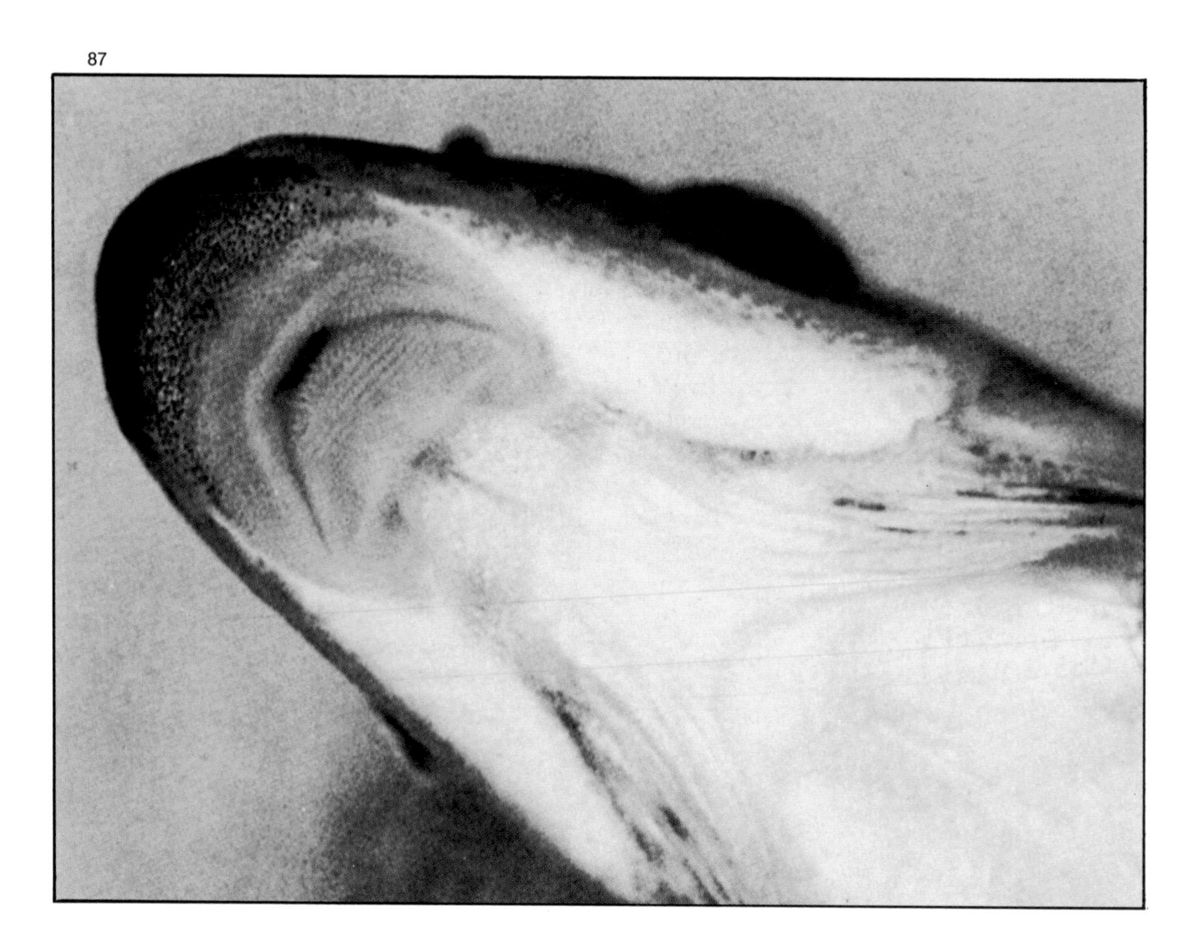

88

and injuring their skin. This can result in the eventual death of the victim since the damaged skin allows dangerous bacteria and fungi to penetrate the body. The young are normally very undemanding and peaceable, but half-grown specimens and adults become quarrelsome and pugnacious. In spite of this, they are frequently imported. Nothing is known about their reproduction, either in the wild or in captivity. *Gyrinocheilus kaznakovi* was for long imported into Europe under the incorrect name *G. aymonieri*. The two species are distinguished by the shapes of their upper lip. While *G. kaznakovi*'s is horseshoe-shaped when viewed from below (see picture 88), *G. aymonieri*'s lip is larger and is pointed in the middle, rather like a V-shape. Only *G. kaznakovi* is reared in aquariums; the published data on the number of fin rays, the number of scales in the lateral line system, and the morphology of the apparatus, formed by gill rakers in the front side of the gill arches, refers to this species, too.

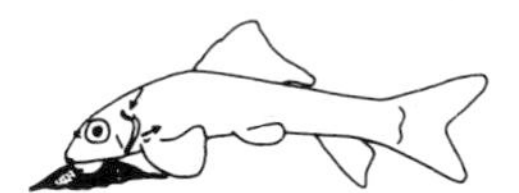

Gyrinocheilus kaznakovi breathing while attached by mouth suction to the substrate.

89

Clown Loach or **Tiger Botia** [89] (*Botia macracantha*)

In Sumatra and south-eastern Borneo this species lives in flowing and stagnant waters. It grows to about 30 cm long but in captivity it is never longer than 15 cm. It has the most beautiful colours of any member of the family. The male is smaller and slimmer than the female and has darker and more pronounced colours. The fins, in particular, are a vivid blood-red. The Clown Loach needs a densely overgrown tank, a soft sandy bottom-soil and crystal-clean water which is not too hard and is rich in oxygen.

Botia macracantha

Cross-banded Loach [90] (*Botia striata*)

This fish comes from Thailand and does not grow beyond 5 cm long. It belongs to the family Cobitidae, whose representatives are distributed throughout Eurasia, from Spain to the Pacific Ocean. Aquarists prefer the species of the genera *Acanthophthalmus* and

Botia. Some representatives of the genus *Acanthophthalmus* have been bred in captivity, but species of the genus *Botia* have not. *Botia striata* needs a medium-size tank with fine and completely washed sand on the bottom. The water must be well-aerated. This fish likes to hide, and lives in shoals. If a small number of specimens is kept, they become shy and quarrelsome.

90

Chapter 3

THE KNIGHTS OF THE WATER BEDS

Hancock's Amblydoras [91] *(Amblydoras hancocki)* is a real knight of the bottom, as its body is covered with a thick armour of transverse bony plates along the sides of the body that protrude into spines.

Many catfish inhabit freshwater bottoms throughout the world. They are well-adapted to the benthonic habitat. Their bodies are naked or covered with a thick armour of bony plates and they are often decorated with bizarre spikes. Together they form the large suborder Siluroidei which includes some 30 families and about 2,000 species. The origin of these naked or armoured knights of the bottom is obscure. They have much in common with characins, on the one hand, and with carps on the other. Their mouth seldom has any teeth. This chapter deals only with the species most interesting for aquarists, the tropical and subtropical representatives of the suborder. These are popular with aquarists throughout the world. The tropical and subtropical forms are mainly members of the family of mailed catfishes (Callichthyidae), thorny catfishes (Doradidae), Loricariidae, Pimelodidae, Pangasiidae, Clariidae, Ameiuridae, and others. Some of them have acclimatized in aquariums. Others, however, refuse to reproduce in captivity and must always be imported from their native environments.

Hancock's Amblydoras [91, 92] (*Amblydoras hancocki*)

Native to the Amazon basin in Peru, Bolivia and Guyana, it grows to a length of 15 cm. The flanks are covered with transverse bony plates, each protruding to form a spine. The fish builds a nest from the plant leaves into which the eggs are deposited. When caught in a net it gives off quacking sounds. The fish seek hiding places at the bottom and feed on bottom fauna, such as the larvae of chironomid midges, tubificid worms and the larvae of various insects as well as on dry food that falls to the bottom.

◀ 91 92

Port Hoplo [93, 94] (*Hoplosternum thoracatum*)

The Port Hoplo is found from Panama to Paraguay. It grows to about 18 cm long. The male is larger than the female and has larger pectoral fins and strongly developed, spiny armour. In aquariums it prefers a low light intensity. The male builds a bubble-nest, usually under a floating leaf. In aquariums a yellow or white water lily, or even a small polystyrene plate, can be used as a nest-carrier. The female attaches about 800 eggs to the underside of the leaf [94]. The male takes care of the eggs. At a water temperature of about 23–24°C the young hatch after approximately four days. If disturbed, the male sometimes eats the eggs or even the hatched fry. The male protects the nesting place and it is therefore advisable to carefully remove the female after spawning.

93

94

Aquarists often keep a close relative, the **Armoured Catfish** (*Callichthys callichthys*), which occurs from eastern Brazil to the Río de la Plata basin. In aquariums the two species have similar requirements but *Callichthys callichthys* is much less prolific. The number of eggs from one spawning is usually less than 120. The fry hatch in 4–5 days. The free-swimming ones stay near the bottom. They like to devour minced tubificid worms, small enchytraeid worms, and tiny *Cyclops* scalded with hot water.

Dwarf Corydoras or **Rabaut's Corydoras** [95] (*Corydoras rabauti*)

The smaller tributaries of the Amazon river near its junction with the Río Negro are the habitat of this species, which grows to a length of about 6 cm. Young fish change their colour twice before it stabilizes when they are about 3 cm long. However, the full-grown specimens also differ according to the locality in which they were caught. It is therefore no wonder that this species is also listed as *C. myersi* and *C. zygatus*.

Schultze's Corydoras [96] (*Corydoras schultzei*)

This also occurs in many small tributaries of the Amazon. The adults are about 6.5 cm long. They have an elongated body with a flat dorsal profile. This hardy fish is easy to breed and rear.

◀ 95

96

Common Bullhead or **Marbled Bullhead** [97] (*Ameiurus nebulosus*)

The Common Bullhead, from the waters of the eastern United States, is about 40 cm long and weighs about 2 kg. In the last century it was imported into Europe and became acclimatized in the basins of the Danube and Elbe. It belongs to the family Ameiuridae. Its body is naked and there is a well-developed adipose fin in front of the caudal fin. In the wild it digs shallow pits in the water bed into which it spawns. The male takes care of the eggs and fry. The Common Bullhead feeds on bottom fauna such as tubificid worms and larvae of chironomid midges and on pieces of fish meat. Only young specimens are suitable for breeding in unheated aquariums.

97

Pimelodus ornatus [98]

This species belongs to the *Pimelodidae*, a family embracing many genera and species distributed from southern Mexico through Central and South America; it is absent only

98

from the extreme south. All species of this family have three pairs of barbels, the maxillary pair being the longest. Many species of the genera *Pimelodus*, *Pimelodella*, *Pseudopimelodus*, *Rhamdia*, *Acentronichthys*, *Heptapterus*, *Sorubim* and *Microglanis* have been imported recently, but breeding in captivity has not yet been successful.

99

Pangasius sutchi [99]

Widespread in Thailand, this species is often imported into Europe. The optimum water temperature for keeping this fish in captivity is 22–28°C. It is very voracious and can detect live food at long range. If it is properly fed it will grow quickly. Nothing is known about the reproduction of this species. It has apparently never suffered from any disease in captivity. Frequent partial water replacement is beneficial for the health of the fish. The family Pangasiidae includes many representatives from southern Asian and Indonesian waters. The genus *Pangasius* has 15 species. *P. sutchi* is only about 20 cm long, whereas the largest are giants among the family and exceed 3 m (*P. sanitwongsei*).

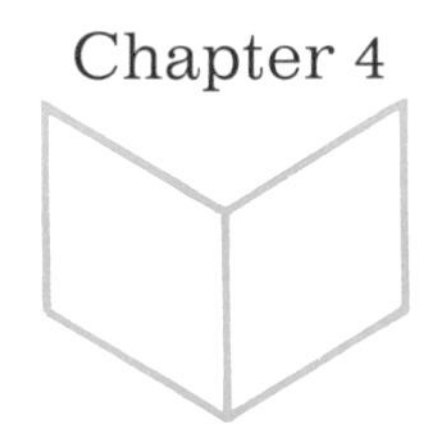

Chapter 4

FISHES FALLING FROM THE SKY

Steel-blue Aphyosemion [100] (*Aphyosemion gardneri*) belongs among the most colourful species of its genus. The fish are undemanding as to the spawning substrate: they will happily spawn on sand or peat, as well as on plants.

The tropics, subtropics and monsoon regions of south-east Asia and the adjacent islands, Africa and South America are inhabited by the egg-laying tooth-carps of the family Cyprinodontidae. They live in flowing and stagnant waters, and even in muddy pools. The adult males of all species are larger and more colourful than the inconspicuous females, which are mostly brownish in colour. The eggs are deposited onto plants or in the sandy and muddy substrate. Sometimes the fishes will modify the spawning substrate according to need. The eggs either develop continuously in permanent waters or, in ephemeral waters, their development may be interrupted by one or more diapauses (periods of spontaneous dormancy). The species with interrupted development are called annual fishes. In the African species the interruption of development is usually shorter and lasts several weeks to months, whereas in the South American species the diapause may last up to two years. When the dry season comes the pools, which are entirely dependent on the supply of rainwater, dry up and the adult fish die. Only the eggs survive in the dry and cracked mud until the next period of rain. The fish do not literally fall from the sky, but rainwater helps to save the species in the most severe conditions. Most of the species are adapted to life in very soft water. As a rule the eggs are either sticky or their surface is covered with various filaments, hooks and threads by which they are attached to the substrate, and the egg cover is tough. About 430 species are known to ichthyologists and many of them are bred in aquariums.

Cape Lopez Lyretail or **Aphyosemion** [101, 102] (*Aphyosemion australe*)

This fish inhabits muddy coastal waters of the Congo and Gabon and grows to 5.3 cm long. It is a peaceable and placid fish and is content in a small and shallow aquarium. Very soft water, e.g. rainwater, is the best medium for breeding this fish. The eggs are laid on fine-leaved plants such as *Myriophyllum*, *Fontinalis*, *Riccia* or *Ceratopteris*. Water temperature may fluctuate between 22 and 24°C. The fry hatch after 12–20 days and immediately begin to swim freely. They greedily take live food such as rotifer and

◀ 100 101

102

brine shrimp nauplii. Their growth is quick. The aquarium must be covered with glass, since all species of the genus *Aphyosemion* are good jumpers. An orange mutant of this fish, bred in aquariums, is known as *A.a. hjerreseni* [101].

Red-spotted Aphyosemion [103] (*Aphyosemion lujae*)

Living in the waters of the middle Congo and its southern tributary, the Kasai, this fish grows to about 5.5 cm long. The male's body colouring is very variable. The conditions needed for breeding this fish are similar to those required by the Cape Lopez Lyretail.

103

The breeding pair spawns on plants. The eggs, which are small (1.3–1.4 mm in diameter), develop continuously. The fry are very sensitive and must be well but carefully fed immediately after they learn to swim. Little success has been achieved in breeding this fish in captivity.

Steel-blue Aphyosemion [100, 104, 105, 106] (*Aphyosemion gardneri*)

This is a widespread species which inhabits waters of virgin forests and savanna in Nigeria and western Cameroon. The male is larger than the female; it is about 6 cm long and has large fins with a blue to green sheen. The male's body is covered with 30 to 90 deep red blotches which are arranged in irregular longitudinal rows. Owing to the variation of body colour, correct determination has been difficult for many years. In recent literature it has been referred to under the incorrect names *A. calliurum calliurum, A.c. ahli* and *A. nigerianum*. In the wild, a large difference in colour pattern exists between the two basic strains, one from Nigeria and the other from Cameroon. Breeding in aquariums is quite simple. The Steel-blue Aphyosemion spawns both on the substrate and on plants. The size of the eggs of some populations varies from 1.0 to 1.5 mm in diameter. The development of the eggs is continuous, with no diapause. At a

104

temperature of 25°C the fry hatch after 12–20 days and immediately begin to swim freely. They are very voracious and take any live 'powder' food of adequate size. The young grow rapidly. The sex distinctions are already pronounced at the age of two to three months and reproduction may be tried at this age. The Steel-blue Aphyosemion

105

106

readily crosses with the Cape Lopez Lyretail (*A. australe*). However, the hybrids are not remarkable for their colour or body shape. They often suffer from various defects in fin shape, such as fusion of the dorsal fin with the caudal and anal fins.

Christy's Aphyosemion [107] (*Aphyosemion christyi*)

This species from the middle Congo grows to 5 cm long. Two populations or strains, with different chromosome numbers (9 and 15), are known to aquarists. If crossed by chance they produce nonviable progenies. This may be the reason for the much discussed difficulty of breeding in captivity. The eggs are small (some are only 1.2 mm in diameter), and their development is continuous.

107

Red-chinned Aphyosemion [108] (*Aphyosemion calliurum*)

A native of southern Nigeria, it grows to about 5 cm long. In aquariums it reproduces easily and the eggs develop continuously. This fish is able to cross both with *A. ahli* and *A. australe*. In aquarist literature it is often incorrectly referred to as *A. vexillifer*.

108

Plumed Lyretail or **Plumed Aphyosemion** [109] (*Aphyosemion filamentosum*)

Its native waters are the periodic pools of south-western Nigeria. The adults are about 5.5 cm long. In nature it spawns exclusively in the bottom soil and its eggs develop with a diapause. If the eggs are incubated without interruption in the aquarium, the fry hatch with difficulty. Better breeding results are achieved if the fish are encouraged to spawn in fibrous peat. Drained peat should be left moist for about 20 days, then flooded with water again. If kept in this substrate, the small eggs (1.3 mm in diameter) yield more fry of higher viability. Food which could rot should not be left in the peat together with the eggs, otherwise the eggs could be destroyed.

Aphyosemion filamentosum

109

110

Walker's Aphyosemion [110, 111, 112] (*Aphyosemion walkeri*)

Walker's Aphyosemion inhabits the virgin forest waters of south-west Ghana and the south-eastern part of the Ivory Coast. The adults are 6.5 cm long. This bottom-spawning fish is a typical annual species with a discontinuous development of eggs which are 1.4–1.5 mm in size. The development of the eggs lasts several weeks. Adults often suffer from fish tuberculosis.

111

112

Red Lyretail or **Red Aphyosemion** [113] (*Aphyosemion bivittatum*)

This fish is very common in Cameroon and Nigeria. It grows to about 5 cm long. The breeding pair spawns in soft, slightly acid water on a bunch of fine-leaved plants. The male is very active and often kills the female. One spawning, which lasts up to several days, produces about 100–150 eggs. The breeding fish must be removed after spawning. The eggs develop continuously and the fry hatch after some 14 days at a water temperature of about 25°C. Spawning can be repeated after three weeks or so, as soon as the female's body cavity is full with eggs. The fish mature at the age of about six months.

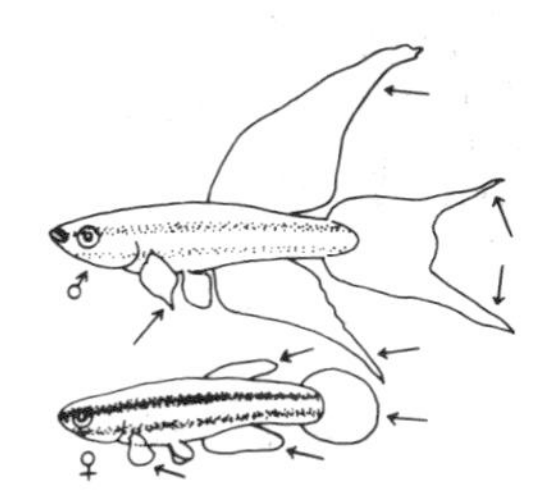

Aphyosemion bivittatum

The Red Aphyosemion has a very variable body and fin shape and body colour, which may be bright brown, yellow, orange, green or blue. Owing to the variability of shape and size and depending on the place of origin, several species, such as *A. multicolor, loennbergi, pappenheimi, riggenbachi, splendopleure* and *unistrigatum*, and subspecies, such as *A. bivittatum holyi*, have been described in the past few decades. By studying the number of chromosomes and by crossing tests, Scheel has demonstrated that these are not true species but are only shape and colour varieties.

113

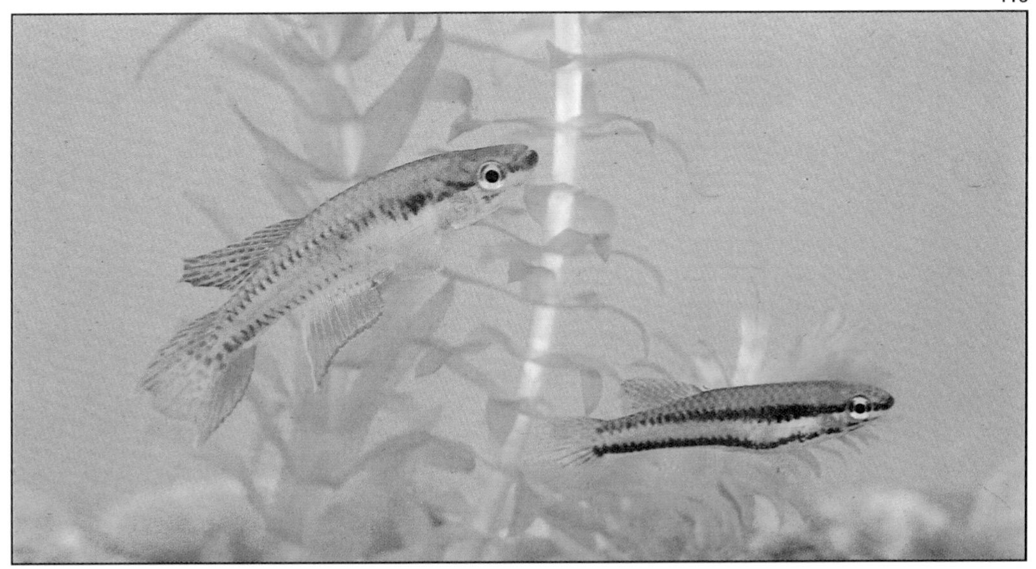

Scheel's Aphyosemion [114] (*Aphyosemion scheeli*)

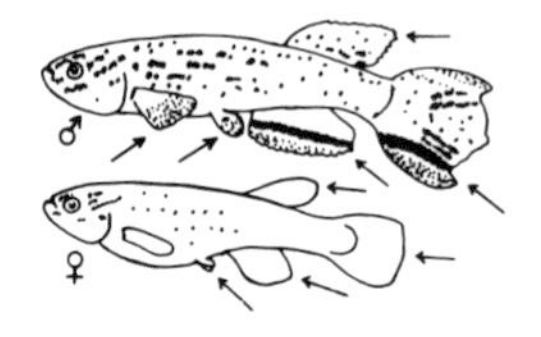

Aphyosemion scheeli

Southern Nigerian waters are the habitat of this fish. The male is about 5.5 cm long. The eggs develop continuously. Breeding is simple and is similar to that of the Steel-blue Aphyosemion. Most aquarists know this species under the commercial name *A. 'burundi'*, which has no nomenclatorial status.

114

Blue Gularis [115] (*Aphyosemion sjoestedti*)

This fish lives in pools in southern Nigeria and western Cameroon. Adults are about 12 cm long. Most aquarists know it under the incorrect names *A. coeruleum* and *A. gulare coeruleum*. The eggs are 1.3–1.5 mm in diameter and their development is discontinuous. The female deposits the eggs in fine sand. If breeding is to be attempted, let the breeding pair spawn in a cylindrical container with sand on the bottom. Stir the sand with a glass rod after a few days so that they collect in the centre of the container. The eggs can then be sucked up easily with a glass pipette. Place them in a petri dish, about 10 cm in diameter and about 12–15 mm deep, and cover with a glass lid. Leave the dishes containing the eggs on a table or in a cupboard at room temperature. Remove the non-fertilized, dead eggs every day to prevent infestation of the developing embryos. The incubation time ranges from three to nine weeks, depending on the temperature; they start swimming freely two to five days after hatching and devour any live 'powder' food. A very small amount of trypaflavin can be added as a fungicide. The water in which the eggs are to develop should have no carbonate hardness, and its non-carbonate hardness should not exceed 5° dNCH. The growth of the young is very irregular. The fast growing specimens must therefore be removed to stop them from eating their smaller siblings. The males usually grow faster than the females. A larger tank with a relatively sparse plant community is suitable for rearing. The fish prefer to stay close to the bottom. The adult pairs are quarrelsome and must be reared separately. Outside spawning time, a temperature of 20°C is required; for the young it needs to be raised to 22°C. They consume only living food, crustaceoplankton, larvae of insects, and water worms.

115

Playfair's Panchax [116, 117, 118] (*Pachypanchax playfairi*)

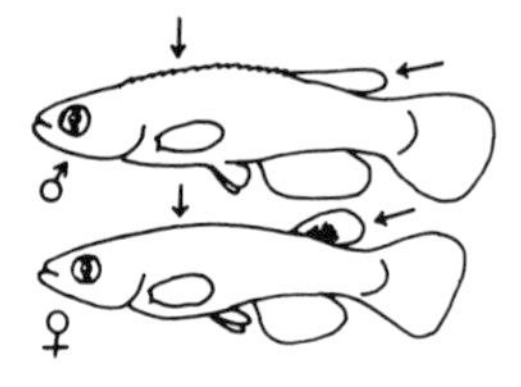

Pachypanchax playfairi

A native of the Seychelles, Zanzibar and various sites in east Africa, it grows to about 10 cm long. The older males often look as if they are suffering from dropsy, since their dorsal scales clearly stand out in spawning time; this is due to hormone activity. The breeding pair stick the eggs to plants. At a temperature of 24–25°C the young hatch after 10–12 days, sometimes a little later. This beautiful fish is quarrelsome and aggressive and it is therefore surprising that although many breeding pairs spawn almost incessantly they do not eat the eggs or the young. The parents can therefore be kept together with the young. The fry grow very slowly.

116

117

118

Géry's Roloffia [119] (*Roloffia geryi*)

This fish inhabits the fresh waters of forests and savannas in southern Guinea and Sierra Leone. The adults are about 4.5 cm long. The male is larger than the female. In both sexes the throat is characteristically red, whereas in the closely related *Roloffia roloffi* the throat is dark. The eggs always develop continuously in aquariums. They are very small, only 0.8 mm in diameter. They develop quickly; at temperatures of 25–27°C the fry hatch after 10–12 days and within a further 24 hours they start to swim and take food. Water hardness for incubation should be about 15° dNCH, with zero carbonate hardness.

119

The fish spawn willingly in the aquarium and are very productive. The male is bigger and more colourful than the female. Its ground colouring is yellowish, greenish to blue-green, with a metallic gloss. Irregular red spots on the body blend with lengthwise zigzag bands. The lyre-shaped caudal fin has golden edges above and below. The red marking on the throat helps identify the species. The female is conspicuously brownish, with a lengthwise dark band on the sides and colourless fins.

Calabar Lyretail [120] (*Roloffia liberiensis*)

Coming from the coastal pools of western Liberia it grows to a length of about 6 cm. It is a semi-annual species (it develops either with or without a diapause in the wild but always develops continuously in aquariums). It is easy to keep and breed in captivity. The breeding pair lay the eggs on fine-leaved plants, in the substrate, or in corners of the tank. The water should be soft and the temperature should range between 24 and 26°C. Under these conditions the young hatch after 14 days. The breeding tank should be well covered since the fishes are very good jumpers and will even try to crawl out of the tank.

120

The Calabar Lyretail is sensitive to sudden changes in water chemistry. The male is larger than the female; his ground colouring is deep blue, with irregular red spots on the body and fins. The dark lengthwise band in the dorsal and anal fins lightens on the outer edges to bluish green. The caudal fin has a golden yellow band at top and bottom. The female is olive brown with a dark spot at the base of the caudal fin; all her fins are colourless.

Sheljuzhko's Panchax [121] (*Epiplatys chaperi sheljuzhkoi*)

This is a subspecies of *E. chaperi*. Both forms live in south-western Ghana and in the Ivory Coast. They grow to about 7 cm long. *E. c. sheljuzhkoi* needs very soft water for breeding, and the pH of the water should be very low. Extremely low pH values (sometimes even 3.5) are known in the natural environment. However, such low pH values cannot be recommended to aquarists since, sooner or later, such acid waters become toxic to practically all other species kept in aquariums. The optimal pH is between six and seven. Breeding and rearing are the same as for *Epiplatys dageti monroviae*.

121

Fire-mouth Epiplatys or **Red-chinned Panchax** [122, 123]

(*Epiplatys dageti monroviae*)

It inhabits the fresh waters of south-western Liberia and it extends eastwards over the swamps to the Ivory Coast. The adults are approximately 5 cm long. The male has an

122

orange to orange-red blotch on the throat; in this it differs from the male of the nominal form, *E. dageti dageti*, which lacks a blotch.

Since it was first imported in 1908, the Fire-mouth Epiplatys has been incorrectly named *Epiplatys chaperi* in aquaristic literature. It is known as a hardy tooth-carp. Small, translucent eggs are deposited on plants. At a temperature of 25°C, the fry hatch after 8 to 10 days. The fry immediately start to swim freely and to take small live food of all kinds. The total water hardness should not exceed 10° dGH.

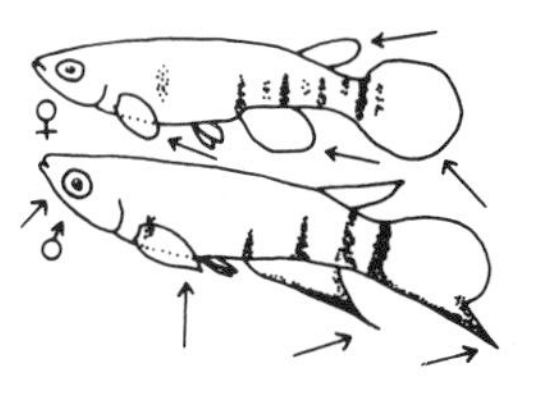

Epiplatys dageti monroviae

123

Banded Epiplatys or **Striped Panchax** [124] (*Epiplatys fasciolatus*)

This species comes from southern Guinea, Sierra Leone and Liberia, and grows to about 8 cm. It has a wide geographical distribution, and inhabits many different types of water. Because of this, the Banded Epiplatys has a very variable body colour and shape. The coastal populations are less colourful than inland specimens and their bodies are more elongate. The Banded Epiplatys lives in the waters of virgin forests as well as in savanna brooks. There are probably a number of so-called sibling species which are

124

hard to distinguish morphologically from one another with certainty. Tests to cross the different populations yield infertile progeny. The spawning tank must be large, with floating plants which give good shelter to the fish. The males are quarrelsome at spawning time. The eggs are about 1.5 mm in diameter. The fry hatch after 12–14 days at 22–24°C. At first, the young keep near the surface. Their growth rate is irregular, making it necessary to sort the fry by size. Throughout their life these fish need medium-soft water with an admixture of sea water or kitchen salt.

Six-barred Epiplatys [125] (*Epiplatys sexfasciatus*)

The Six-barred Epiplatys is native to the waters of virgin forests from eastern Ghana to southern Gabon. The adult specimens are about 10 cm long. The Six-barred Epiplatys, like the Banded Epiplatys, is easy to breed, but the young are very sensitive to changes in the water. They are also susceptible to bacterial fin rot. This is a long-living species and attains its most splendid body colours in the second year of life.

125

126

Guenther's Nothobranch [126, 127] (*Nothobranchius guentheri*)

This fish occurs in central Africa. About 20 species of the genus *Nothobranchius* are known today and most come from southern and eastern Africa. Their bodies are comparatively deep and the scales on their heads and flanks are provided with fine denticles. The eggs are covered with attachment processes. Most of the species are hard to breed in captivity. Medium-hard water at 20–24°C is recommended. In soft water the fish suffer from tuberculosis and dropsy, and are attacked by ectoparasites (mostly *Amyloodinium*). Their productivity is high. The adults are omnivorous. The eggs develop discontinuously, preferably in peat. The fry of some species hatch after four to eight weeks; in other species incubation may last for half a year or longer. The young grow surprisingly quickly: if given enough food they reach sexual maturity at the age of three to four weeks. The exact determination of the species kept in captivity is difficult.

127

Beira Nothobranch [128] (*Nothobranchius melanospilus*)

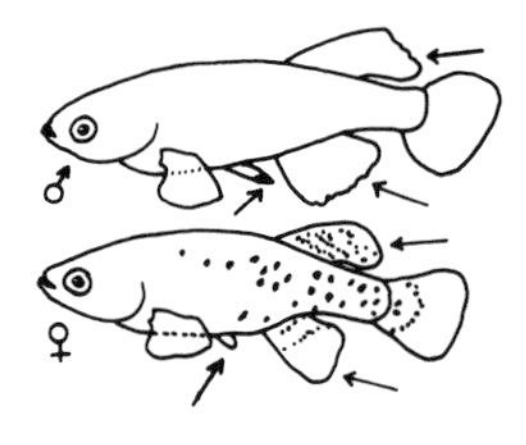

Nothobranchius melanospilus

This is a close relative of *Nothobranchius guentheri*. The female's body is irregularly marked with black dots. The fish comes from mainland Tanzania and the adult specimens are about 7 cm long. Breeding requirements are similar to those for *Nothobranchius guentheri*. These fish are bottom-spawners; their eggs are about 1.5 mm in diameter and they incubate in peat for six to eight weeks.

128

Rachow's Nothobranch [129] (*Nothobranchius taeniopygus*)

Rachow's Nothobranch belongs to a group of sibling species which lives around Lake Victoria in Kenya and in Tanzania; it also extends southwards to Zambia, Zimbabwe, Shaba (Zaïre), and Mozambique. The fish does not grow longer than 5 cm. It spawns in the substrate and the discontinuous development of the eggs lasts some four to six months. The tooth-carps of this group are very sensitive to changes in water composition and to other factors which have not yet been identified in detail. The outcome of breeding this species is therefore uncertain.

129

Green Nothobranch [130, 131] (*Nothobranchius korthausae*)

Found as recently as 1972 on Mafia Island off the coast of Tanzania, it lives mainly in permanent waters. The adult specimens are about 5 cm long. The fish is easy to breed. The eggs develop both continuously and discontinuously, depending on environmental

130

conditions. The breeding fish spawn readily in thickets of plants, in sand, detritus, peat, in the corners of the tank or even on an empty glass bottom. Most of the breeding fish do not eat the eggs. If the eggs are left in water they develop continuously at temperatures of 25–26°C and yield young after 18–21 days. If deposited in damp peat the eggs develop discontinuously over four to six weeks. The fry which hatch from discontinuously developing eggs are much more viable. Water hardness can range between 1 and 15° dGH without any harm to the adults, eggs, or embryos.

131

Striped Aplocheilus [132, 133] (*Aplocheilus lineatus*)

Widespread in India and Sri Lanka, this tooth-carp grows to a length of about 12 cm. It can be kept in tanks only with larger fish since the older individuals are very quarrelsome and voracious. They can easily swallow a fish as large as a female of *Brachydanio rerio*. Breeding and rearing are very simple. The eggs are deposited on the fine-leaved plants *Myriophyllum* or *Riccia*. The young hatch after 14–17 days in water of 24°C. With plenty of food of suitable size the young grow quickly. The young fish are comparatively placid.

132

Species of the genus *Aplocheilus* are distributed from India and Sri Lanka through Thailand and south to the Malay Peninsula. They mainly inhabit forest waters. The females have a dark blotch at the base of the dorsal fin and transverse bars on flanks. They tolerate a wide range of water composition. Many species can be kept in hard water of alkaline reaction. Total hardness can be up to 20° dGH, but carbonate hardness should not be higher than 7° dCH. If carbonate hardness of the water is higher, many embryos die before hatching. All species spawn on plants for several weeks in succession. The daily yield of a fully mature pair is 10–20 eggs covered with a very hard and sticky shell.

133

Blue Panchax [134] (*Aplocheilus panchax panchax*)

The Blue Panchax lives in the waters of the Indian subcontinent, Sri Lanka, and the Indo-Malay Archipelago. The adults grow up to 8 cm long. This tooth-carp is very quarrelsome, aggressive and intolerant of fish of the same species as well as of other species. Its eggs are large, 1.6–1.8 mm in diameter. Coloration is variable and depends on the place of origin.

Selective breeding has produced varieties which have been incorrectly classified as separate species, such as *A. lucescens* and *A. mattei*. The subspecies *A. p. siamensis* has a fine red colour. It lives in Thailand and aquarists know it as *A. rubropunctatus*, which is not a scientifically valid name.

134

Lamp-eyed Panchax [135] (*Procatopus similis*)

This fish is distributed in virgin forest waters from southern Benin to the estuary of the river Niger. Its body is up to 7 cm long. These fish like to assemble in schools and can be successfully bred in aquariums. The breeding fish spawn for several days in succession. The eggs, about 1.5 mm in size, hatch in 10 to 14 days. The fry prefer very fine, live food, such as rotifers. In aquariums the young always grow very slowly, however good the food may be; this is why the productivity of this species is so low.

Aplocheilichthys macrophthalmus (see drawing) belongs to the subfamily Procatopodinae, which includes many genera and species that live in tropical and subtropical Africa. A few species are found in South Africa and in Egypt. All these fish are good swimmers and move in a characteristic 'trembling' fashion. In their natural habitat they live in flowing waters of brooks and rivers. They are not easy to breed in aquariums since flowing water must be at least partially substituted by intensive aeration. The fish stay permanently in the air stream bubbling through the water in the tank. They are sensitive to water composition and cannot live in excessively soft and acid water; even a low nitrite content is toxic to them. Hence the tanks must be perfectly clean and the water should be highly oxygenated. Some peat extract and an admixture of sea salt or kitchen salt are beneficial.

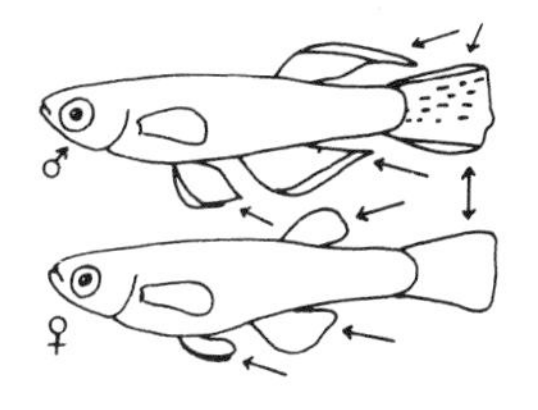

Aplocheilichthys macrophthalmus

135

Colombia Rivulus [136, 137] (*Rivulus milesi*)

This is a native of the basin of the Río Magdalena in Colombia and grows to a length of 6 cm. The large eggs are about 1.9 mm in diameter. Hoedeman doubts that *Rivulus milesi* is a true species; according to him it is most probably a hybrid between *R. elegans*, *R. cylindraceus* and/or *R. urophthalmus*.

The representatives of the genus *Rivulus* are distributed from the Yucatán Peninsula (Mexico), Florida and Cuba throughout Central America and the northern part of South America to the southern regions of Brazil. Taxonomic determination is often very

136

difficult, owing to the adaptation of a large number of species to various environments and the very small interspecific differences. Perhaps Hoedeman's system of identification, which is based on the shape and number of scales on the front and top of the head, is the clearest of all even though this system includes some intermediate forms of uncertain systematic status. Many of the 50 species of the genus *Rivulus* so far known are imported and kept in aquariums. All of them are good leapers and they are often seen stuck to the leaves of plants above the water surface or to the glass walls of the tank. Rearing of most species is easy in pure, medium-hard water. Aeration is not required, but the water must be filtered.

137

Ladiges' Gaucho [138] (*Cynopoecilus ladigesi*)

It comes from northern Uruguay and grows to a length of about 4 cm. It lives in ephemeral waters. The fish deposit their eggs in the bottom-soil and cover them with the substrate by jerking their body and fins at the end of each spawning act. The eggs develop discontinuously. They have a non-adhesive cover which is divided into hexagonal sections with palmately branching peg-like processes. The male has the same number of fin rays in the dorsal and anal fins as the female.

138

Cynolebias whitei [139]

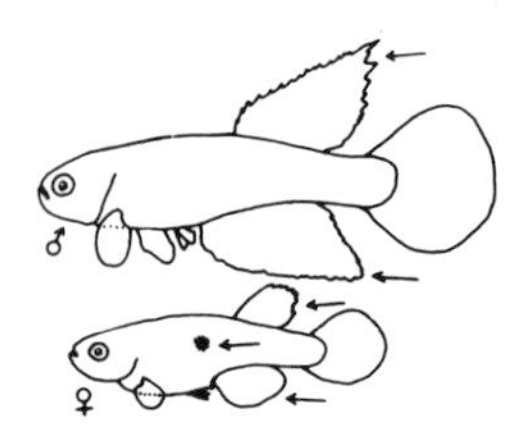

Cynolebias whitei

This species lives in Brazil in the neighbourhood of Rio de Janeiro. The male is about 8 cm long when adult, the female only about 5.5 cm. During the spawning act, the female tucks her head under the male's huge pectoral fin. In this position the urogenital papillae of both fishes are closest to each other. The eggs are laid on the water bed and are buried fairly deep in the substrate where they develop discontinuously. The adult fishes die soon after spawning since their native pools dry up during a dry season. When rains flood the half-dried mud in the pool the fry emerge from the eggs.

139

Black-finned Pearl Fish [140, 141] (*Cynolebias nigripinnis*)

The Black-finned Pearl Fish lives in the basins of the Río de la Plata and the Paraná and especially upstream of Rosario in Argentina. It does not grow longer than 4.5 cm. In its natural habitat it lays its eggs into fine loamy or clay mud which never dries up. In aquariums the eggs can be kept alive for up to three years in mud covered with a thin layer of water.

140

141

Many representatives of the genus *Cynolebias* live in the waters of South America, from the northern regions of Argentina to the estuary of the Amazon. The males have more rays in the dorsal and anal fins than the females; in this they differ from the members of the genus *Cynopoecilus*. About thirty species of *Cynolebias* are known so far. They lay their eggs in the substrate. Only seven species are popular among aquarists.

142

Peruvian Longfin [142] (*Pterolebias peruensis*)

Coming from the Loreto region of Peru on the upper reaches of the Amazon, it grows to 9 cm long. Its mode of life resembles that of the *Cynolebias* species. All the known species of the genus *Pterolebias* inhabit the savanna waters of Peru, Bolivia, Venezuela and Brazil. Their body is slim and the base of the dorsal fin is comparatively short. The dorsal, anal and caudal fins of the male are elongated. All species are bottom-spawners. Dark, fine sand or peat and plenty of floating plants are the best spawning substrates. Three to five species are occasionally kept in captivity.

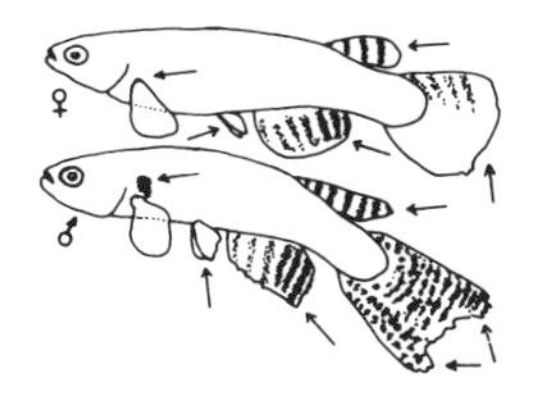

Pterolebias peruensis

143

Venezuela Killifish [143] (*Austrofundulus transilis*)

It lives in the Orinoco basin, Venezuela. The adult specimens are 7.5 cm long. They are robust, aggressive and unsociable and require soft water and plenty of room to swim about. They readily spawn into the bottom soil. The eggs (1.5 mm in diameter) develop discontinuously in five to six months. The breeding pair is very prolific and produces up to 500 eggs or more within a week.

Representatives of the genus *Austrofundulus* inhabit the savanna creeks of east Venezuela and Colombia. They are similar in appearance to the African fishes of the genus *Nothobranchius*. Only five species are known. *A. dolichopterus, A. transilis* and *A. myersi* have been kept by aquarists. *A. dolichopterus* is the smallest of them and only grows up to 5 cm long, whereas *A. myersi* reaches a length of 13 cm.

Chapter 5

THE LIVE-BEARING FISHES

Red Platy [144] (*Xiphophorus maculatus* var. *sanguinea*) is one of the most favoured mutants bred in aquariums. It is appreciated for its bright blood-red colour and size, and also for the porcelain-white borders of its fins.

The southern United States, the West Indies and the countries of Central and South America down to northern Argentina are inhabited by many live-bearing tooth-carps (family Poeciliidae). They live in various fresh and brackish waters. Sexual dimorphism is typical. The anal fin of the male is transformed into a copulatory organ known as the gonopodium. The largest species are no longer than 20 cm. The males are usually smaller than the females. Young are produced several times a year. The number of young per brood varies with the species and ranges from just a few to several hundred. The newly born young are fully developed and immediately capable of living independently. The female can bear several times from one fertilization.

Live-bearers living in captivity need plenty of plant and animal food. The females of many species are cannibalistic and must be separated from the young immediately. This can be done by keeping the pregnant female in a brood-cage from which the young fall through a narrow slit in the cage and so are out of the reach of the mother. Soon after delivery the young start hunting for live 'powder' food as well as dry and artificial food. Their growth is rapid. In genetic tests, or in breeding the best-coloured specimens, the young should be divided according to sex as soon as possible and the males and females should be reared apart. Most species tend to produce xanthoric and albino forms and these mutants are selected for aquarists.

'Wagtail Swordtail' [145] (*Xiphophorus helleri*)

This is a mutant of splendid colour and shape and is artificially produced in aquariums. The ground colour can be green, red or white and characteristic traits are a beautifully developed dorsal fin in the male and smoke grey to black fins in both sexes.

◄144 145

'Tuxedo Swordtail' [146] (*Xiphophorus helleri*)

The 'Tuxedo Swordtail' is another cultivated strain, with black body sides and a splendid green-silver sheen. The ground colour is grey-green, red or white.

146

'Lyre Swordtail' [147] (*Xiphophorus helleri*)

This fish also represents the achievements of aquarium culture. The males have a 'sword' on both the upper and lower lobes of the caudal fin. The caudal fin of the female has the same shape. A sword-like process is found on the dorsal fin as well, and the pelvic fins are also long. Usually the gonopodium is exceptionally long and highly flexible. The males often fail to copulate and the breeder must fertilize the female artificially to save this splendid mutation. The ground colour of these fish is green, red or white.

147

There is a number of other interesting mutations [148] besides the three mentioned above. All are derived from the wild Swordtail (*Xiphophorus helleri*) which has almost been forgotten by aquarists. Its native land is southern Mexico and Guatemala. The females grow to a length of 12 cm. The males are smaller and the lower caudal fin rays are elongated to produce a black-edged sword. The ground colour of the wild form is grey-green with a reddish longitudinal band extending from the snout to the base of the tail. Breeding in captivity is simple.

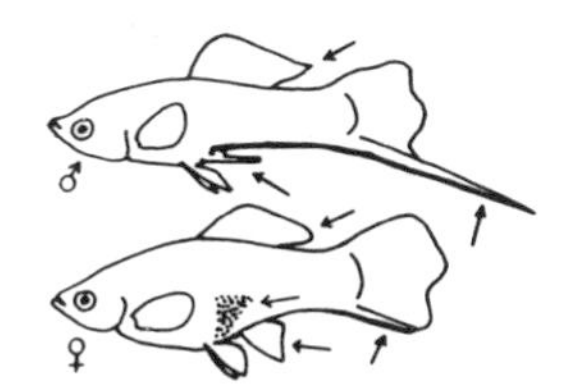

Xiphophorus helleri

Plenty of room and food should be provided for the fish throughout the year to allow them to grow to a sufficient size before reaching sexual maturity. In bad conditions they produce dwarf forms but this is not a genetic problem related to long-term inbreeding. Rather, the dwarfs develop as a result of a high concentration of nitrogen compounds in the confined space of the aquarium.

148

'Meri-gold Platy' [149] (*Xiphophorus variatus*)

This is one of the most beautiful mutants of this species that has been bred in captivity. The front part of the male's body is orange and it has a lemon-yellow back and dorsal fin. The hind part of the body, including the tail fin, is blood red. These thermophilic fishes are hard to breed. The broods contain up to 50 per cent of non-fertilized eggs. A similar mutant, perhaps the loveliest of all, is called the 'Parrot Platy'. The males are rainbow-coloured with a metallic sheen.

149

'Red Platy' [144, 150] (*Xiphophorus maculatus* var. *sanguinea*)

The typical feature of this cultivated strain is its bright red colour. The males are blood red and appreciated for the porcelain-white borders of their fins. These, like other colour mutations of the wild platy (*Xiphophorus maculatus*), have low genetic stability. *Xiphophorus maculatus* comes from Mexico and Guatemala. The female is larger than the male and grows to 6 cm in length. Its original colour is brown to olive, with a blue sheen and with two black oval blotches on the caudal peduncle close to the base of the tail fin. A blotch also lies on both flanks behind the gill covers. Various colour and shape mutations have been developed in aquariums. These artificially cultivated forms, unlike the wild fish, are specially sensitive to water temperature. Platies are tolerant to varying water composition but the pH should be slightly alkaline. They are not choosy and can be fed any live or dry foods, plant fragments, algae and so on. The brood, usually up to 100 young, is generally delivered in the early hours of the morning. The young are easy to rear and can be fed dry or artificial food. The optimal temperature for breeding this fish is between 20 and 26°C.

150

151

'Comet Platy' [151] (*Xiphophorus maculatus*)

This fish is a popular colour mutation with a red or yellow ground colour. The body of both sexes is covered with the same characteristic design: two black stripes, one lining the upper and the other the lower edge of the caudal fin. Neither the wild platy nor the cultivated strains have a sword; in this they differ from the swordtails. The differently coloured mutants must be kept separately in aquariums, otherwise long-term selection work would be spoilt by crossing.

'Tuxedo Platy' [152] (*Xiphophorus maculatus*)

This robust and deep-bodied strain usually has a yellow or red ground colour which is only visible on the belly and fins. The flanks are black with a splendid metallic green lustre. Individuals of this strain are resistant and genetically stable if they come from high-quality stocks.

152

'Calico Platy' [153] (*Xiphophorus maculatus*)

The 'Calico Platy' is a strain with very variable ground colours from yellow through green, brown and orange to red; it is irregularly sprinkled with numerous darker spots of varying size and shape. The fish of this mutation are smaller and slimmer than other platies.

153

In general, platies are undemanding and can be recommended to beginners. At the same time, they provide valuable genetic material and are appreciated by advanced aquarists who use them in intensive breeding experiments for obtaining new forms or for keeping the existing strains stable and improving their show qualities. Great patience is needed for such work, which can last many years and even then does not always lead to success. Much credit is due to the American geneticist M. Gordon, who has studied the genetics of platies for many years and has produced several strains. The 'Wagtail Platy', for instance, is a successful product of his laboratory. Apart from the platies already described there are monotone strains of yellow, blue and even black.

154

Guppy [154, 155] (*Poecilia reticulata*)

The Guppy inhabits the waters of Venezuela, the islands of Barbados and Trinidad, northern Brazil and Guyana. The female grows to a length of 6 cm, the male only to 3 cm. It was brought to Europe in 1908. The fish has become a highly appreciated object for genetic observations and experiments because of the great colour and shape variability, particularly in the males. Aquarists have developed many cultivated strains and these have provided magnificent showpieces for aquaristic exhibitions. The show specimens are evaluated according to international standards. One of the most variable traits is the shape of the male's dorsal and caudal fins, of which 11 basic types are known. Females with splendidly coloured and strongly developed fins [155] have recently been developed. At water temperatures between 22 and 25°C pregnancy lasts about 30 days. The pregnant females have a dark 'pregnancy mark' on the back part of the belly. One fertilization by the male will suffice for two to three broods or more. The males are typically polygamous and very active. The young are delivered within two hours, depending on the water temperature, its chemical composition and freshness, and on the environment, particularly the fish community. Wanting to protect the young, the female may delay parturition by several hours, or at least retard it. One brood contains up to 250 young.

155

Sail-fin Molly [156] (*Poecilia velifera*)

This species is distributed in the coastal regions and river estuaries of the Yucatán Peninsula (Mexico). In aquariums it grows to 12 cm; in its natural habitat to about 15 cm. The males have a remarkably prominent dorsal fin. Many mutants of beautiful

156

shapes and colours have been bred in captivity. This species has also been crossed with *P. latipinna* and *P. sphenops*. The best-known of these mutations and crossbreeds are the 'Black Mollienesia', 'Lyre Mollienesia' and 'Veil Mollienesia'. Breeding and rearing in captivity is difficult, owing to genetic instability and rigid requirements for good living conditions and food (plenty of plant food and a temperature of about 28°C).

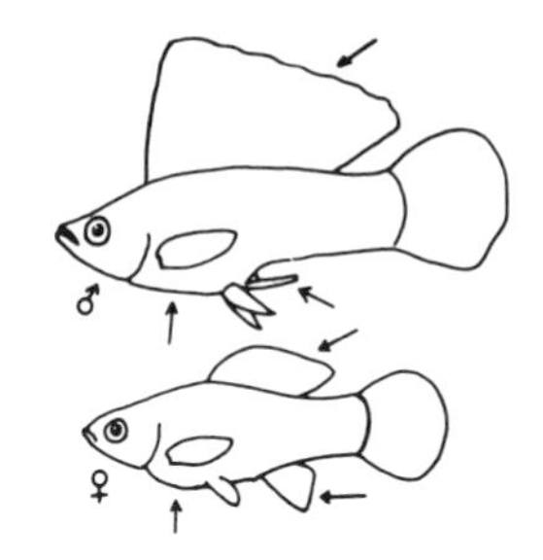

Poecilia velifera

157

Pike Top Minnow [157] (*Belonesox belizanus*)

This largest live-bearer of the family *Poeciliidae* inhabits the waters of the eastern part of Central America. The female grows to a length of about 20 cm, whereas the male is only half that size. It is a predator and is unsuitable for community tanks. Before copulation, the male turns his gonopodium forwards and strangely twists and bows his body. Feeding is not simple. Adult fish need large pieces of live food such as small fish, dragonfly larvae, tadpoles, and worms of all kinds. Specimens of 10–20 cm length can swallow full-grown female platies or guppies without difficulty. Their upper jaw is movable and this allows the fish to swallow large pieces of food. Water temperature should be kept between 25 and 30°C. A point of interest is their ability to change colour. The fishes are dark at night and lighter during the day. The brood contains up to 100 young, 2.5–3 cm long, which immediately start feeding on small daphnia and enchytraeids. The mothers often greedily devour their own young or at the least will harass them brutally.

158

The golden breeding forms of **Amazonian Scalar** [158] (*Pterophyllum scalare*) look beautiful in an aquarium richly overgrown by green plants.

Chapter 6

MONOGAMISTS WITH A REFINED SENSE OF FAMILY LIFE

Perch-like fishes (Perciformes) represent a large group of bony fishes living in marine, brackish and freshwater habitats. The fish of this order usually have two dorsal fins; the first consists entirely of hard spiny rays whereas the rays of the other are soft and branched. The pelvic fins lie below the pectorals. The scales are mostly ctenoid. This order includes many suborders and families. Three of these families which show a well developed sense of care for the young are of interest here. These are the cichlids (Cichlidae), the nandus-fishes (Nandidae) and the sunfish and basses (Centrarchidae). Together, these three families are distributed in North, Central and South America and in Africa and south-east Asia. They lay their eggs on plant leaves (phytophilic species), into small pits in sand (psammophilic species), on flat stones (lithophilic species), or into crevices. The young are cared for by the male or female, or alternately by both. Mouthbrooders show a very special kind of care; the lower part of the male's or female's mouth acts as an incubator for the eggs and a hiding place for the young in the first few days of their life.

159

Cichlasoma spilurum [159, 160]

This fish comes from Guatemala. The male [160] is larger than the female and grows to a length of about 10 cm. This species spawns in caves, a habit which, as some authors believe, is exceptional among species of the genus *Cichlasoma*. However, another species of *Cichlasoma*, the Zebra Cichlid, also prefers caves as spawning places. The fry of *Cichlasoma spilurum* hatch at 25–26°C after three days and the female carries them in her mouth into a pit in sand. After another three days the fry start to swim freely and eat live 'powder' food. Their growth is rapid. The adults are peaceable and look stately. They cause no damage to plants in the aquarium. Outside the spawning season they do not dig the bottom sand at all.

160

161

Zebra Cichlid or **Convict Cichlid** [161, 162, 163] (*Cichlasoma nigrofasciatum*)

The Zebra Cichlid also comes from Guatemala, from the Atitlán and Amatitlán mountain lakes. It is smaller than *Cichlasoma spilurum*; the males, which are larger than the females, grow to be about 8 cm long. The male has markedly elongated dorsal and anal fins. The hind part of the female's belly has a shining bronze colour throughout its life. A xanthoric form with black eyes has been developed in aquariums. In a shaded tank this milk-coloured mutation is particularly conspicuous among green plants. A female with the bronze coloured belly is shown in picture 161.

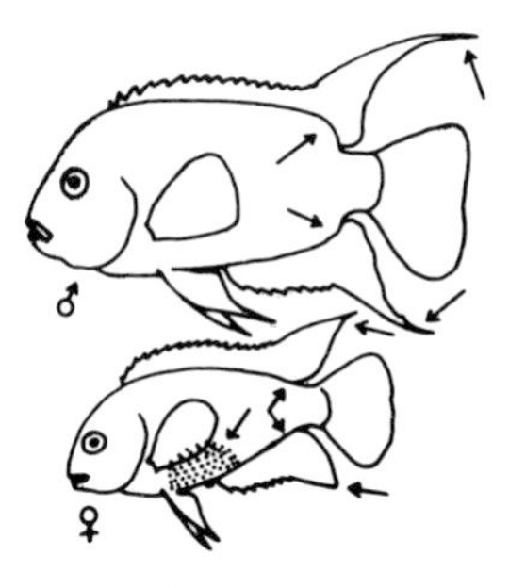

Cichlasoma nigrofasciatum

162

The original wild form of the Zebra Cichlid is brightly coloured. It is very aggressive both to other species and individuals of its own kind. In aquariums it keeps grubbing up and rebuilding the tank bed and often destroys plants in the process. It will also nibble and bite them. They can be fed lettuce, soaked oat flakes, algae and the like. Meat must be provided as the basic food. The breeding pair will spawn in a pile of stones or in an old flower-pot. Sometimes a flat stone may suffice. The Zebra Cichlid has an unusual behavioural pattern designed to protect the young. When the fry hatch, the parents immediately transfer them to a small pit excavated in the sand or among stones. The parents change the hiding place if the environment is disturbed. The actual transfer of the young is both sophisticated and complicated. One of the parents tries to attract attention by engaging in very conspicuous activity, such as digging a pit in the sand in an open place. While this decoy activity is going on the other parent carries the fry to another safe place. The parents are brave when defending their young or eggs against intruders which have come close to the hiding place. In picture 163 a Zebra Cichlid attacks the aquarist's finger without fear. The other breeding and rearing conditions are the same as in the previous species.

163

Hybrid between ***Cichlasoma nigrofasciatum*** x ***C. spilurum*** [164]

This hybrid has been known for several years and the offspring are fertile. The hybrid displays an intermediate colour and can be clearly distinguished from both parent species. Crosses between *C. spilurum* and the xanthoric form of *C. nigrofasciatum* result in weak progeny which never reach maturity. The breeding pair spawn and the embryos develop normally until the free swimming stage, but the young are never able to fill the swimbladder. Sometimes the young suffer from constitutional dropsy which soon kills them. Sometimes they will keep moving sluggishly, jumping on the bottom and even accepting food, but eventually they die. In crosses of this type two females often spawn together, one behaving like a male on one day and changing roles the next. Such pairs of females produce many eggs but naturally nothing can hatch from the non-fertilized eggs and they soon decay. The females often fight with each other, each characteristically holding the other's mouth [164].

164

Barred Cichlid or **Flag Cichlid** or **Festivum** [165] (*Cichlasoma festivum*)

This species inhabits the waters of western Guyana and the Amazon basin. The male, larger than the female, grows to 15 cm long. Sex distinctions are almost absent; the male can be distinguished only in the breeding season by the shape of the genital papilla which is conical and pointed, whereas in the female it is cylindrical and is uniform in diameter throughout its length.

According to data in aquaristic literature this fish is peaceable, shy, and does not destroy the water plants. However, this is not true at spawning time, when the fish quickly devastate anything they can, leaving only the remains of plants. When preparing the spawning place in the aquarium, the breeding pair removes large stones and pieces of wood. The sandy substrate is gradually transformed into numerous heaps and pits reaching down to the glass bottom. These vigorous preparations are usually followed by quiet spawning on a flat stone or flower pot. Both parents look after their young with great care from the very beginning. Having learned to swim, the young can be fed the finest 'powder' food such as rotifers. If given coarser food (for example, nauplii of *Cyclops*) 90 per cent of them die within two to three days. The young and adults are warmth-loving and require temperatures between 25 and 28°C.

165

Brown Discus or **Yellow-brown Discus** [166]

(*Symphysodon aequifasciatus axelrodi*)

Coming from the waters of Brazil, it grows to the length of 12–15 cm. It is difficult to breed and rear in captivity. Both young and adults have strict requirements for water quality, clean and varied food, and for cohabitants. It is recommended that this species be kept alone. They often suffer from diseases which are hard to treat with success. The fry need very careful attention from hatching to sexual maturity. During the first few days after hatching the fry feed on a dermal secretion produced by their parents and only later do they start eating normal 'powder' food. If the parents do not start producing the dermal secretion in time the young die. Some success has been recorded with the use of food replacers in recent years but such feeding is difficult, complicated and very time-consuming.

166

167

Blue Discus [167] (*Symphysodon aequifasciatus haraldi*)

The upper Amazon basin, especially the waters around the towns of Leticia and Benjamin Constant, are the habitat of this fish. Except for the middle part of the flanks the whole body of the fish is longitudinally crossed with brilliant blue wavy bars which also cover the dorsal and anal fins. The head is decorated likewise. The iris of the eye is bright red. In Europe the Blue Discus has been successfully bred and reared in captivity for several years. It occasionally cross-breeds with the Brown Discus. The naturally occurring **Red Discus** (*S. discus*), **Green Discus** (*S. aequifasciatus*) and its subspecies, **Brown Discus** (*S. a. axelrodi*), and Blue Discus all enjoy high popularity among aquarists.

Newly discovered wild forms and artificially developed strains are also popular and are marketed under commercial names such as 'Royal Blue Discus', 'Cobalt Blue Discus', etc.

Flag Cichlid [168] (*Aequidens curviceps*)

It comes from the Amazon basin and grows to about 8 cm long. It is a peaceable fish which can be kept in community tanks outside the breeding season. The young breeding pairs usually devour the eggs from the first spawning after a day or two. Further spawnings are normal and the parents take exemplary care of their eggs and young. The Flag Cichlid belongs to the lithophilic species; that is, it spawns on flat stones. Before spawning the parents carefully clean the stone with their mouths. The female lays the eggs alone; then she leaves the stone to let the male fertilize them. The female has a thick tubular or cylindrical ovipositor, whereas the urogenital papilla of the male is conical and pointed. The number of eggs laid on a stone gradually increases. The male swims around the female and keeps any uninvited guests away. Both parents share equally the protective duty and can replace each other in all post-spawning functions. The best rearing temperature is 26°C. The tank should be of medium size and have a sandy bottom.

Red Cichlid or **Jewelfish** [169] (*Hemichromis bimaculatus*)

Living in large populations in the drainage basins of the Nile, Congo and Niger rivers, it inhabits fresh as well as brackish waters. The adult individuals are about 15 cm long. The male is larger than the female. The back of the fish is olive to grey-brown with yellow-green flanks and a yellowish belly. At spawning time this fish is perhaps the most splendid African cichlid. The male takes on a rich red colour with shiny green dots all over the body. The front part of the body of some females is sulphur yellow and the back part is red. In other populations the females are bright red all over the body [169].

169

Borelli's Dwarf Cichlid [170] (*Apistogramma borellii*)

This cichlid inhabits a large region of South America from the Mato Grosso southward to Argentina via the Río Paraguay basin. It grows to a length of about 7.5 cm. The male is larger than the female. The fish is very thermophilic and water temperature should never be lower than 22°C. In smaller aquariums the fishes spawn in separate pairs, whereas in their natural habitat and in larger tanks they probably spawn in groups. The young male always keeps with a single female, whereas the older male spawns with several females at the same time and defends a territory which would otherwise belong to more pairs. According to Wickler the older males do not treat the young males as rivals but only protect their territory against outside attacks.

Breeding and rearing of the young is difficult. The younger parents sometimes swallow the first few broods of eggs. At a temperature of about 26°C the young emerge within two to four days. After another five to six days they consume all the nutricious yolk and start swimming freely. They associate in a shoal, keeping close to the female for some two to four weeks. At first the young should only be given fine live food such as rotifers but later they can be offered *Cyclops* nauplii and adult *Cyclops* and *Daphnia*. They grow quickly.

170

Yellow Dwarf Cichlid [171] (*Apistogramma reitzigi*)

Its native waters are in the central part of Paraguay. The adults grow to about 5 cm long. The male, which is larger than the female, has huge dorsal and anal fins. The back of the fish is green-grey, the flanks are grey-yellow and the belly is bright yellow. If the fish are content, their body sides have a bluish sheen. These fish are best bred in soft water with slightly alkaline reaction at a temperature of about 26°C. The brood number is small.

171

172

Amazonian Scalar [158, 172] (*Pterophyllum scalare*)

This fish lives in the central Amazon basin and its tributaries. It grows to 26 cm in height, while it is only 15 cm long. It requires a high-sided tank and a minimum water temperature of 22 to 24°C, rising to 27–32°C for rearing and breeding of the young. It feeds on *Daphniae* species, larvae of chironomid midges (*Chironomus*), tubificid worms (*Tubifex*) and fish fry. In aquariums many mutants have been selected and bred. Among the most admired are black, black veil, smoke veil, ordinary veil, albinos, xanthoric, silver, gold [158], orange and the various marble colours [172].

173

Eartheater or **Demon Fish** [173] (*Geophagus jurupari*)

Living in waters with sandy bottoms in the Amazon basin and in Guyana, it associates in shoals and the individuals grow up to a length of 23 cm. Despite their aggressive appearance the fish of this species are peaceable. They do not dig in the substrate and do not destroy well-rooted plants. Both in the wild and in captivity they keep chewing the detritus from the bottom soil, taking anything edible. The Eartheater prefers food of a small size, such as *Daphnia*, tubificid worms and larvae of chironomid midges. Even during winter the temperature in the tank should be kept at 22°C. The fish prospers best at 25–28°C.

Ramirez's Dwarf Cichlid [174, 175] (*Papiliochromis ramirezi*)

This popular aquarium fish comes from the Río Apure and Río Meta in Venezuela. The male is larger than the female and grows to about 7 cm long. As distinct from the fish of the genus *Apistogramma,* the body of Ramirez's Dwarf Cichlid is deep and strongly compressed on the sides. *Papiliochromis ramirezi* represents an intermediate form between the genera *Apistogramma* and *Geophagus*; the structure of its eggs is similar to those of the latter, whereas the remaining characteristics are similar to those of the genus *Apistogramma.* The main difference between the genera *Apistogramma* and *Papiliochromis* is in the position of the lateral line. The ground colour of Ramirez's Dwarf Cichlid is purple and changes by incident light. The flanks, including the fins, are covered with shining green to blue spots. The upper part of the iris of the eye is a brilliant light blue, the front part of the dorsal fin is deep black. The first three spinous dorsal fin rays of the male are markedly elongated. Breeding and rearing are similar to that of *Apistogramma* species.

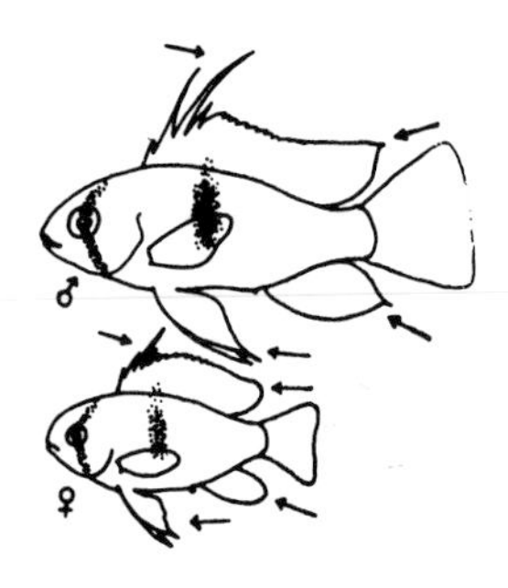

Papiliochromis ramirezi

The breeding pairs prefer stones as the spawning place, but a pit in the sand may serve just as well. Brood care is undertaken alternately by both parents. Each spawning yields 150–200 eggs. *P. ramirezi* is a beautiful fish but unfortunately it rarely lives longer than two years. It requires clean water and suffers from many incurable diseases, such as dropsy and fish tuberculosis. Its cultivated xanthoric strain [175], which has the same requirements as the type species, has become popular in recent years.

174

175

Badis [176] (*Badis badis*)

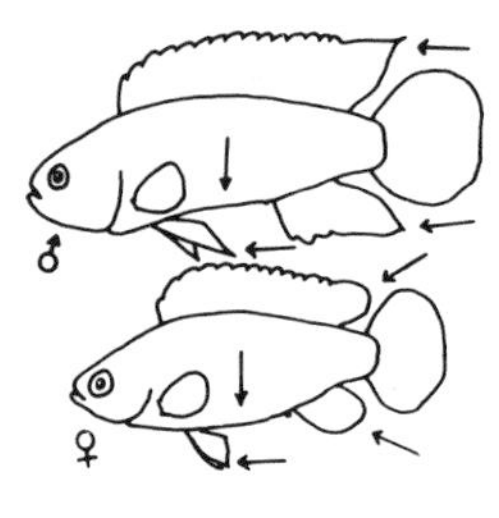

Badis badis

The Badis inhabits stagnant waters in India and grows to a length of about 8 cm. The male is usually larger than the female and his body is arched. The mouth of these fish is relatively small. *Badis badis* is the only species of the family Nandidae suitable for community tanks, as it is placid and peaceable. It needs water temperatures between 26 and 28°C. The tank should provide hiding places under stones and roots, or dense thickets of aquatic plants. The fish accept all kinds of live food. In the spawning season the males display their outstretched fins and the dorsal fin is often erected. The eggs are laid in a hollow among stones or in a flower pot. The male takes care of the brood.

176

Oscar's Cichlid or **Velvet Cichlid** [177] (*Astronotus ocellatus*)

This is a large cichlid coming from the waters of the Amazon, Negro, Paraná and Paraguay rivers. It grows up to 35 cm long. The young have particularly splendid colours, marbled with chocolate brown in various shades with irregular black-edged markings. These 'youthful' colours disappear with increasing age and size, until a uniform brown-grey body colour is left. The tank must be large enough to suit the size of the fish. Oscar's Cichlid is unsuitable for a community tank. Every day it consumes a large amount of live food (flour worms, crickets, earthworms, pieces of lean beef, horse or poultry meat) in large pieces.

One spawning may yield more than 1,000 young, which are carried about attached to the flanks of the parents during the first days of life. The young seek protection and perhaps also their first food, a dermal secretion, as in the discus fishes.

Owing to the wide distribution of the species, fish from different localities are differently coloured. Recently a splendid red strain known as the 'Red Oscar' has been bred in aquariums and has aroused the interest of aquarists. Unlike the wild species, the adults retain their splendid red colour.

177

178

Pumpkinseed Sunfish [178] (*Lepomis gibbosus*)

A species of the family Centrarchidae, it is distributed in North America from Dakota to the Mexican Gulf. In the wild it grows to about 20 cm long; in aquariums it only reaches 10–12 cm. It has acclimatized not only in aquariums but also in ponds and open waters, for instance in the drainage basins of the Danube and Elbe. The fish builds dish-like pits in sand, which is the best spawning substrate. It is able to survive the winter in unheated aquariums without difficulty. The fish accept only live food. Breeding and rearing are simple.

179

Maria's Tilapia [179] (*Tilapia mariae*)

Abundant in West Africa, mainly in the lower basin of the Niger and around Lagos, it grows to a length of about 15 cm. It is exclusively herbivorous in its natural habitat, where it eats stands of aquatic plants. It spawns in hollows excavated by the females under stones. After about two days the female picks the eggs from the ceiling of the crevice and transfers them to a pit previously excavated in sand. The young emerge soon after this transfer. Having learned to swim, they feed on live 'powder' food. The breeding temperature should be kept between 25 and 27°C.

180

Chromidotilapia kingsleyae [180]

This fish comes from southern Gabon and is up to 25 cm long. The eggs develop in a throat sac in the male's mouth. Although it is very similar to *Chromidotilapia guentheri*, the cichlid expert Thys van den Audenauerde considers them as two separate species. The picture shows a female.

181

182

Herotilapia multispinosa [181, 182, 183]

This species is native to Central America where it lives in Lago de Managua in Nicaragua and in the small rivers of Guatemala, Panama and Costa Rica. The male grows to a length of about 12 cm and its belly is flat; in this it differs from the female which is smaller and has a rounded belly. The spawning season lasts three to four months and the fish lay 800–1,000 eggs at three- to four-week intervals. The eggs are tough and orange in colour. If laid on glass they can be removed with a razor blade and transferred to an all-glass tank for further development without great losses. Spawning follows after courtship displays, preferably at 24–27°C. The breeding pairs seek the darker places of the tank for spawning. They stick the eggs to stones, into a flower pot or coconut shell, onto plant leaves, or on the glass walls of the tank just above the bottom. Picture 183 shows a male over the eggs. Water should be slightly acid (pH 6) and with a hardness of up to 15° dGH. The parents incessantly clean the eggs with their mouths and fan them with their fins. The fry hatch after five days and the parents transfer them into a pit in the sand. They begin to swim freely within another five days. At this stage the parents can be removed and the young fish can be given 'powder' food.

If the water is kept pure, the young grow quickly up to a length of 1.5 cm. Their growth then markedly slows down. The characteristic body colouring [182] appears when the fish is about 5 cm long (at the age of six months). It reaches sexual maturity at the age of about nine months. Pronounced transverse bars indicate deterioration of health which may be due to long-lasting exposure to low temperatures (below 20°C).

183

Five-spot African Cichlid [184] (*Thysia ansorgei*)

It lives in large populations in the fresh and brackish waters of Nigeria, Ghana and the Ivory Coast. The adult male is larger than the female and reaches a length of about 13 cm. Best breeding results have always been obtained from those pairs which left the shoal by themselves. They prefer to spawn into flower pots, on overhanging slate plates or coconut shells. Both parents share duties of caring for the brood. The eggs are large and light brown in colour. The young hatch after three days and begin to swim freely after seven days. The water temperature should be about 26°C. Live and artificial food can be given to these fish.

The species is sometimes known as *Pelmatochromis annectens* and *P. arnoldi*, which may also be encountered in the literature, but these are scientifically invalid synonyms. In picture 184 the female is laying the eggs, whilst the male waits to fertilize them.

184

Red Dwarf Cichlid or **Kribensis** [185, 186, 187] (*Pelvicachromis pulcher*)

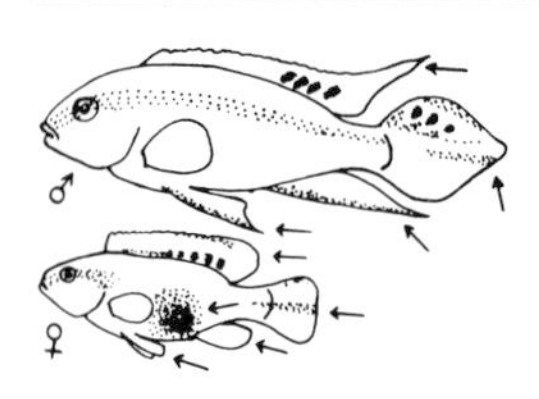

Pelvicachromis pulcher

This fish is a native of the tropical waters of West Africa, especially the estuary of the Niger. The male grows up to a length of 10 cm, the female only to 7 cm. The water temperature must be kept at 25–28°C for successful breeding. Adult specimens require a supplement of vegetable food in their diet. The parents share the brood care. They like to hide their eggs in shelters such as a flower pot. The eggs are red-brown in colour. The breeder should transfer the eggs to all-glass tanks with slightly aerated water.

The fry hatch within two to three days and learn to swim in another four to five. If the aquarium does not offer suitable hiding places the fish build shelters under

185

stones and among the roots of plants. They are incompatible with other fish of their own kind and should be kept in separate pairs. The species *P. pulcher* has two colour mutants known to aquarists under the names *P. kribensis* and *P. aureocephalus*. The sexes can easily be distinguished; the male's caudal fin is lanceolate, whereas that of the female is straight-edged.

Other species of the genus *Pelvicachromis* are also available. *P. subocellatus* and *P. taeniatus* are splendidly coloured and are very popular among aquarists. Breeding and rearing are basically the same in all species.

186

187

Orange Chromide [188] (*Etroplus maculatus*)

The Orange Chromide inhabits the fresh and brackish waters of southern India and Sri Lanka. It grows up to 8 cm long. In aquariums it is very sensitive to any change of water. It is frequently attacked by external parasites, particularly by *Ichthyophthirius multifiliis*. Treatment is difficult because the Orange Chromide is very sensitive to chemicals and drugs. Heavy invasion by the parasite *Ichthyophthirius* kills the fish. Some resistance to the disease is obtained if 1–2 teaspoons of sea salt per 10 litres of water are added to the aquarium. In tanks with adult specimens the temperature of water should be no lower than 25°C. The fry should not be kept in water colder than 27°C. Reproduction is the same as in all lithophilic cichlids. The eggs are laid on stones. The brood care is undertaken jointly by the female and the male. After hatching, the fry remain attached to the parents for some time, as in discus species (*Symphysodon*). However, the young fish can also be reared separately if fed live 'powder' food of adequate size. Hence the fry do not depend entirely on the dermal secretion of their parents. The close mother/fry relationship usually lasts a long time.

The orange Chromide is one species of the only Asian genus *Etroplus*. The other species, the **Green Chromide** (*E. suratensis*), is also well-known to European aquarists.

188

Astatotilapia burtoni [189]

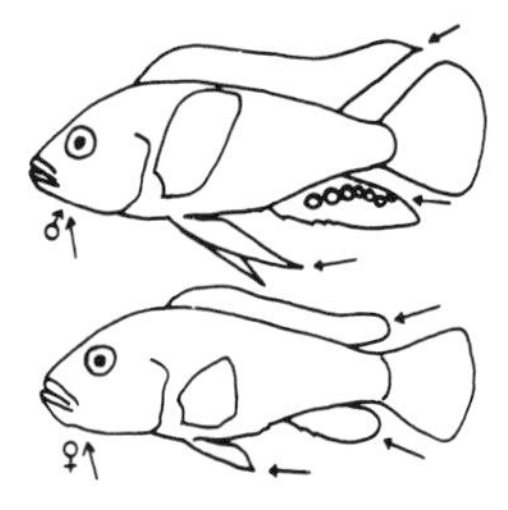

Astatotilapia burtoni

This species inhabits the tropical waters of eastern and central Africa and the northern reaches of the Nile basin. Adults grow to a length of 12 cm. Confrontations between the partners are common during the courtship displays if the eggs of the female are still unripe. It is therefore useful to provide numerous shelters and hiding places in which the weaker female can escape from the attacks of the male which is eager to spawn. The optimal breeding temperature is 27°C. The pair needs plenty of live food, tubificid worms, larvae of chironomid midges and so on. This species has a very interesting method of securing complete fertilization of the eggs. Before the female lays the eggs the male lies on his side on a cleaned stone. He bends his body and ejects the milt while shivering all over. The female approaches with her head to the male's anal fin and tries to pick the egg-like colour pattern from the fin while she sucks the sperm into her mouth. Then she lays a small batch of eggs on a stone and takes them into her mouth (the throat sac) and sucks the male's milt again. The whole process of spawning lasts about an hour and a half. At a water temperature of 26–27°C, the eggs develop for sixteen to twenty days in the female's throat sac. Fully developed fry then leave the mother's mouth. The female offers the young the shelter of her mouth in time of danger and at night. This interesting behaviour lasts for a period of about a week.

Similar breeding habits can also be observed in other African mouthbrooders, such as *Haplochromis desfontainesi*, which is distributed all over North Africa.

189

190

Thomas's Dwarf Cichlid [190, 191, 192] (*Anomalochromis thomasi*)

This cichlid comes from the waters around Kenema in south-eastern Sierra Leone. The male, which grows up to 10 cm long, is larger than the female. In its general appearance this species resembles *Papiliochromis ramirezi.* Its body colours are splendid and very variable. The adult males are grey-green and have a shining blue mark on each scale. Three dark blotches, one on the gill cover, another in the middle of the flanks and a third at the base of the tail, complement the body colours. The blotches are indistinct on the flanks and give way to seven transverse bars, the first of which crosses the eye obliquely. The dorsal fin is fringed with red and has a shining golden margin. The upper lobe of the caudal fin is also rimmed with red. In the male

191

192

the dorsal and anal fins are strongly produced and the pelvic fins have blue or black leading edges. *A. thomasi* lays green-grey eggs on a flat stone which has been cleaned in advance. The brood number is about 500 eggs. This undemanding African cichlid is content in water at 23–25°C but higher temperatures may speed up the development of the eggs and young. At 28°C the fry hatch within 48 hours and begin to swim freely after another three days. The young, which eat live 'powder' food, are easy to rear.

Southern Mouthbreeder [193] (*Pseudocrenilabrus philander dispersus*)

This cichlid is widely distributed in Namibia, the Transvaal (South Africa), Zimbabwe, Rhodesia, Angola and southern Zaïre. The male, which grows up to 11 cm long, is larger than the female. Water temperatures between 24 and 26°C are needed for breeding. Adult specimens, however, survive temperatures as low as 20°C. They prosper best in fresh, medium-hard water of a neutral reaction. To prevent the male from killing the female at spawning time the female must be carefully chosen and trouble is avoided if the female is filled with eggs and ready to spawn. The eggs are laid into a small pit which has been made in the sand by the male. After fertilization the female places the eggs into her throat sac, in which they can be seen as they get darker, particularly in the latter stages of development. It is recommended that the male be removed immediately after spawning to prevent him from disturbing the female. The development of the eggs in the female's mouth lasts 10–12 days. The fry which leave the mother's mouth are about 6 mm long. They are immediately able to swim and seek food. At night, or in times of danger, the young find refuge in their mother's mouth. While she keeps the young in her mouth the female does not eat; she moves slowly, breathes with difficulty and is shy. The number of eggs laid at each spawning depends on the size of the female and ranges between 30 and 100. Rearing is easy.

193

194

Pseudotropheus auratus [194]

The rocky coast of Lake Nyasa (Lake Malawi) in East Africa is the home of this fish. The male, which is larger than the female, grows to a length of 11 cm. The male's ground colour is brown-black to blue-black; the female's is golden yellow with longitudinal bars. The body colours of this fish are very pronounced and conspicuous. The fish feed on algae and supplement this diet with tubificid worms and *Daphnia*. The female hatches the eggs in her mouth. Fully developed young, 1 cm long, leave their mother's mouth after 22–26 days.

195

Pseudotropheus zebra [195]

This is also a native of Lake Nyasa, but is larger than the preceding species; the male grows up to 15 cm long. It likes to stay among rocks in its natural environment and among stones in the aquarium. It is an omnivorous species which feeds not only on algae but on all kinds of food. It acclimatizes easily to aquarium conditions. The fish of this species are quarrelsome and each specimen occupies a comparatively large territory in nature. This implies that they are only suitable for large aquariums. The female hatches the young in her mouth.

Ring-tailed Pike Cichlid [196] (*Crenicichla saxatilis*)

This species occurs in large populations in Trinidad, in the central and eastern part of the Amazon basin and in southern Brazil. In the wild it grows to 35 cm long. In captivity it is much smaller. The tanks for spawning should be as large as possible. The breeding pairs spawn in shallow pits in sand. Brood care is the male's task but the females need not be removed. The whitish eggs are very small. The adult fishes greedily devour small fish, larvae of dragon-flies, various water worms and pieces of lean meat. Water temperature should not drop below 20°C. Depending on their age and

196

197

where they were caught, individuals of *C. saxatilis* may differ markedly in colour. The adult fish is quarrelsome and belligerent, and needs to be reared in a big tank, ideally in the company of large cichlids.

Melanochromis brevis [197]

It comes from Lake Malawi and does not grow to more than 6–7 cm in length. It is quarrelsome but skirmishes never lead to serious injuries. The ground colour is glossy brown with a bluish sheen. The males have a marked orange blotch on their anal fin. The aquarium should be large, holding 50 litres or more, and the bottom should be rocky. The fish must be kept in crystal clear, hard and alkaline water at temperatures of 25–28°C. Young and adults are very sensitive to pH values under 7 and to increased quantities of nitrites in the water. They need live food, but pieces of meat or TetraMin and TetraPhyll are also accepted. Spawning females are easily recognized by the sacs on the lower part of their mouths. Such females should be carefully transferred to a small glass tank with intensive aeration. The separated females should not be given any food because they cannot eat with their brood in the mouth. The eggs develop for about 17 days. The young are very shy at first and quite independent. The fry are about 8 mm long. The colour of the fry is the same as that of the adults. Rearing is simple and easy.

Labidochromis coeruleus [198]

Another native of Lake Malawi, in captivity grows to a length of 7–8 cm. It is quarrelsome but skirmishes do not lead to serious wounds in either party. The water in the tank should be crystal clear, hard and alkaline, free from nitrites and warm (25–28°C). The males are azure blue and their pelvic fins are conspicuously long and are bordered with black. The orange blotches on the anal fin are much more pronounced in the females than in the males. The blotches are even absent from some males. The females are much smaller, inconspicuous and grey-blue. The eggs are brooded in the female's mouth. Breeding is similar to that with *Melanochromis brevis*. The eggs develop for about 20 days and the young leaving their mother's mouth are 1 cm long, independent and they tend to escape from the mother. The brood number is low. The fry should be fed with live 'powder' food. Rearing is easy. The adult fish do not form territories; they live either separately or in pairs, and are among the most peaceable Mbuna-cichlid species. They eat live food as well as frozen or dried foods in flake or tablet form. In nature they are found at depths of 2 to 40 m, and live on rocky substrates as well as in stands of the water plant *Vallisneria aethiopica*.

198

199

Limnochromis auritus [199]

This is a native of Lake Tanganyika (between Tanzania and Zaïre) where it grows to a length of about 19 cm. It is peaceable and shy. The water should be crystal clear, hard, alkaline and warm (25–28°C). The fish eats any live food, preferably large pieces of earthworms or meat. In the wild it lives at depths from 5 to 125 metres. In captivity the activity of the fish increases at dusk. During the day they spend most of their time hidden in shelters among stones. Although fish of this species remain voracious in captivity, their health deteriorates after a long time and all attempts to breed them have so far failed. It requires a large tank with hiding places, such as caverns of stones, or petrified tree roots. The bottom should be sandy. Alkaline medium-hard water is best and it needs to be partially replaced frequently. *L. auritus* is a typical ovophile mouth-breeder, and both partners incubate the eggs in the mouth. They take turns to incubate, and exchange the eggs from mouth to mouth. As many as 300 young are produced at each egg-laying. *L. auritus* is a monoform species; the male is hard to distinguish from the female, though in older males the ventral fins are longer. The species has been reared in captivity since 1958, and was previously known as *Paratilapia aurita* and *Pelmatochromis auritus*.

Chapter 7

THE FOAMY CRADLE FOR THE YOUNG

The male of the red breeding form of **Dwarf Gourami** [200] (*Colisa lalia*) watches over the foamy nest filled with eggs. The nest is supported by floating plants, and is defended fearlessly by the male.

Labyrinth fishes (Anabantidae) are widely distributed in fresh waters of south-eastern Asia and in the tropical zone of Africa. They are believed to have evolved from the same ancestors as the perches. Anabantids have become adapted to life in shallow, often muddy waters which are usually poor in oxygen. To survive in such an unfavourable environment they have a labyrinth, an additional respiratory organ, which enables them to obtain atmospheric oxygen.

The body of these fish is covered with ctenoid scales. The dorsal and anal fins are supported by spines in the front parts. At spawning time some of the labyrinth fish build a foam nest just beneath the water surface or deeper in the water under the leaves of aquatic plants. This nest, into which the eggs are deposited, is built from air bubbles which are surrounded by a hardened secretion from the oral mucous membrane. The male undertakes the care of the brood alone. Many species are successfully kept and reproduced in aquariums.

Three-spot Gourami [201, 202, 203] (*Trichogaster trichopterus*)

This species comes from the Malay Peninsula, Thailand, southern Vietnam, and the Greater Sunda Islands of Indonesia. It grows up to 15 cm. It includes many colour varieties. The most popular among them is the **Blue Gourami** (*T.t. sumatranus*) [203]

◄ 200

201

202

from Sumatra, which is variable in colour; the cultivated strains are golden [201, 202], silver or marbled. The latter are known under the commercial name *T. trichopterus* 'Cosby', after the successful breeder who initiated and stabilized this form. The wild form of the Three-spot Gourami is less demanding for warmth than all its splendidly coloured cultivated strains. Apart from this the main requirements for care in captivity are generally the same in all forms. They reach sexual maturity when about 7–8 cm long. The male drives the female before pairing and builds the foam nest just beneath the water surface. The fish constantly change their body colours during courtship. When the male feels that the nest is firm enough he tries to entice the female under the layer of bubbles. The female with ripe eggs follows him and once under the nest the fish stop and stand side by side with their mouths somewhat raised. The female is embraced from the side and rotated onto her back [202]. The fish then quiver for a moment and jerk abruptly, and a cloud of eggs and milt is ejected. After the act both fish fall towards the water bed. The eggs, which contain numerous oil droplets, ascend to the surface. The male collects the eggs and spits them into the nest. When spawning is over the male adds new layers of bubbles to the underside of the nest and drives the female away, sometimes vigorously. The female should therefore be cautiously removed at this stage to avoid disturbance of the male during brood care. The fry hatch after about three days at a water temperature of about 28°C. One spawning sometimes yields more than 1,000 very small young. They should be fed with rotifers at first and nauplii of *Cyclops* in later stages of growth. The respiratory labyrinth does not develop in the young fish until the age of three to four weeks, when they start breathing the air at the water surface. It is very important at this stage to keep the temperature under the covering glass the same as in the water otherwise the fry 'catch cold' and soon die.

Besides this species with beautiful cultivated strains, other gourami species are also kept in aquariums. Some of these are the **Moonlight Gourami** (*T. microlepis*) and the **Snake-skinned Gourami** (*T. pectoralis*), which are far less splendid than all forms of the Three-spot Gourami. These two species spawn quietly and peacefully. The Snake-skinned Gourami takes care of the young for a very long time and never attacks or threatens the fry of other fish, however small they may be.

203

204

205

Pearl Gourami or **Mosaic Gourami** [204, 205, 206, 207] (*Trichogaster leeri*)

Coming from the waters of the Malay Peninsula, Thailand, Sumatra and Borneo, it grows to a length of about 11 cm. It is very peaceable, shy and warmth-loving. At spawning time the male usually builds a large bubble nest which is wide and high. Spawning, breeding and rearing are generally the same as in the Three-spot Gourami.

206

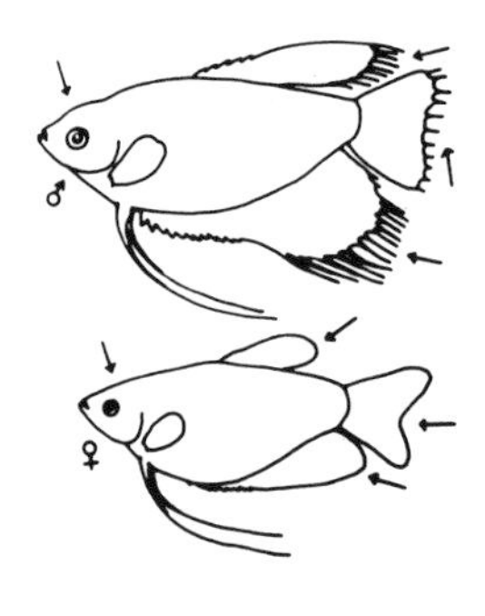

Trichogaster feeri

It must be emphasized that the fishes of the genus *Trichogaster* must be given plenty of live food and that the composition of the diet must be varied. *Cyclops, Daphnia,* larvae of chironomid midges, gnats and mayflies are the best food. Long-continued feeding with tubificid worms, particularly in the winter season, often leads to fatalities. An unsuitable diet not only encourages the transmission of infections but may also support the development of infectious dropsy (the ulcerous form) and fish tuberculosis. Both diseases are hard to treat and sometimes kill large stocks which would be otherwise kept successfully.

207

208

Siamese Fighting Fish [208, 209, 210] (*Betta splendens*)

This fish is widely distributed in the Malay Peninsula and Thailand. The adults are up to 6 cm long. Populations from Thailand and Vietnam are mostly green; those from Singapore are red. The gill cover of the Siamese Fighting Fish is always red. Longfinned forms of various colours have been developed through artificial selection. At spawning time the male builds a comparatively large nest, about 10 x 10 cm in size. The courtship displays take place near the nest and are full of splendid movements. The male displays the splendour of his outstretched fins. This display behaviour lasts for varying lengths of time, depending on readiness to spawn. Mating itself takes place under the foam nest. The eggs ejected by the female are heavier than water and slowly fall to the bottom. Immediately after each spawning act the male picks up the eggs and

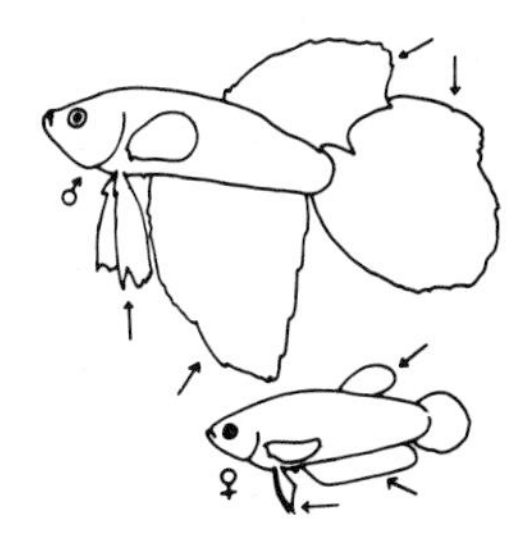

Betta splendens

209

spits them into the nest. The female often helps him. Later, the male drives her away from the nest. He continues adding further layers of bubbles to the nest from below, thus building the eggs into the nest. When spawning is complete the female must be removed, otherwise the male might bite her to death in the small space of the breeding tank. The fry hatch at a water temperature of 27 or 28°C within 24–36 hours, and are carefully tended and protected by the male. They are best fed with live 'powder' food such as rotifers, nauplii of *Cyclops* and brine shrimp. Growth is rapid and at the age of five to six months the fish are fully developed and ready to reproduce.

In their native countries, the male Siamese Fighting Fish are used like cocks in cock-fights in public contests. In captivity numerous cultivated varieties of *Betta splendens,* differing in colour and shape, have been developed. The most popular specimens combine splendid colouring with well developed dorsal, caudal and anal fins.

210

Pacific Fighting Fish [211] (*Betta imbellis*)

This is found only in one locality in India and in the area of Kuala Lumpur (Malaysia), where it was discovered as recently as 1970. It grows up to 5 cm. The gill cover is always green. This very shy labyrinth fish only shows the splendour of its colours in a shaded tank in the company of fish of its own kind. The males try hard to intimidate one another but this never leads to serious injury. The spawning behaviour is the same as that of the Siamese Fighting Fish, but whereas the latter lays 500–800 eggs at one spawning, female Pacific Fighting Fish will rarely produce more than 200. The eggs of *Betta imbellis* are large and the fry are robust but clumsy at the beginning, feeding only on the finest grade and very gradually turning to food such as infusorians and rotifers. They are able to swallow the nauplii of *Cyclops* and brine shrimps after four to six days of free swimming. Their growth is also very slow. The young fish do not usually reach sexual maturity until eight to nine months. They require comparatively soft water up to about 6° dGH, carbonate hardness not exceeding 1° dCH and a neutral water pH value. In contrast to the Siamese Fighting Fish, *Betta imbellis* is a very good leaper and can jump as high as 20 cm above the water surface. If the tank is not tightly covered the fish literally crawls up the corners and passes through incredibly narrow slits between the edge of the tank and the cover glass.

211

The feeding habits of this species are also different; it does not throw itself greedily upon food, but approaches it reluctantly, turns it over in the mouth, spits it out and takes it in again several times before swallowing it.

Thick-lipped Gourami [212] (*Colisa labiosa*)

The Thick-lipped Gourami comes from southern Burma. The male, which is larger than the female, grows to a length of 8 cm. The eggs are kept in a nest on the water surface. They contain large quantities of fat which makes them float. Breeding and rearing are the same as in the Three-spot Gourami. Water temperature should be kept at 27–30°C. The male's dorsal fin has a red margin and the anal fin is rimmed with white. The body is strongly compressed on both the sides.

212

Giant or **Striped** or **Banded Gourami** [213] (*Colisa fasciata*)

A close relative of the Thick-lipped Gourami, this is a native of India and Burma, where it lives in muddy waters and grows to a length of 12 cm. The water in the tank should be kept at 24–28°C. Higher temperatures (up to 30°C) are recommended for spawning and for rearing the young. However, adult fish can withstand temperatures as low as 15°C. They are not choosy about food. The Giant Gourami differs from its thick-lipped relative in the whitish rim on the dorsal fin and red rim on the anal fin. Its body is cylindrical and elongated.

213

Colisa chuna [214]

The smallest of all the gouramis is a native of north-eastern India. Its body is only 4–4.6 cm long. Many colour modifications of this species are known to exist due to its wide distribution in nature. In addition, a golden strain has been cultivated artificially. Breeding in captivity is simple. The pairs spawn at the comparatively low temperature of about 24°C. The brood number is small, ranging from 150 to 250 young. The fry must be fed the finest live 'powder' food in the first one or two weeks. Perhaps rotifers are the best food since the youngest fish have trouble in catching jumping *Cyclops* nauplii. Immature fish and females have a broad brown longitudinal band on their flanks which is a clear distinguishing feature.

214

Almost all *Colisa* species are very susceptible to disease (*Amyloodinium* and infectious dropsy). Like fish of the genus *Trichogaster,* species of *Colisa* are most susceptible to disease in winter when fed tubificid worms over a long period of time. *Colisa chuna* is an exception.

Paradise-fish [215, 216, 217] (*Macropodus opercularis opercularis*)

The Paradise-fish comes from the waters of Korea, China, southern Vietnam and Taiwan. The male is up to 9 cm long. Water temperature of 15 to 20°C is sufficient for keeping this fish, but for breeding the water should be warmer (20–24°C). The Paradise-fish is a quarrelsome species, unsuitable for community tanks. Fasted specimens are used by aquarists for controlling planarian-worms in the tanks. A purebred red-eyed albino form [216, 217] has been known since the 1940s. Although it looks attractive in the tank, it has never been very popular among aquarists. It is advisable to give the fish plenty of food immediately before spawning. The male builds the foam nest for several hours or days, depending on the partner's readiness to spawn. While working on the nest the male keeps driving the female away but when his work is finished he tries to entice her under the nest. He swims close to her, displays his outstretched fins and slowly returns to the nest, watching to see whether the female is following. If she is willing to spawn the two fish lie side by side, heads to tails with their heads turned slightly upwards and then they slowly turn until they become closely pressed to each other's flank. The male embraces the female and turns her upside down; both fish shiver for a moment and then a small cloud of eggs is ejected by the

215

216

female [216]. When the act is finished, both parents slowly fall to the bottom. The male is the first to recover and he collects the eggs and spits them into the foam nest. The spawning act is repeated many times at various intervals until the female has ejected all the ripe eggs. When spawning is complete the female should be removed as the male alone takes care of the brood. Rearing is similar to that of the Three-spot Gourami, with the exception that the Paradise-fish does not require such fine live 'powder' food.

217

Black Paradise-fish [218, 219] (*Macropodus opercularis concolor*)

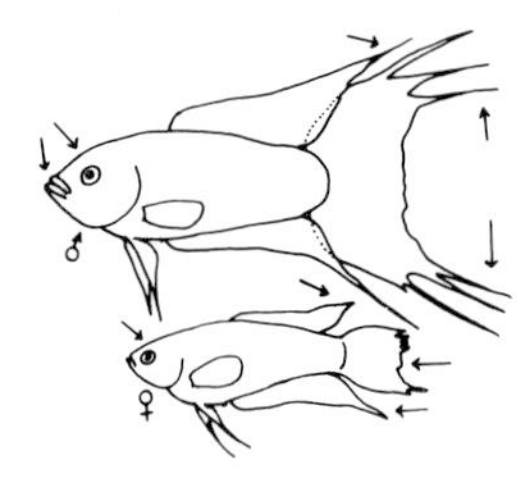

Macropodus opercularis concolor

This is a native of Indochina where it grows to about 10 cm long. It is distinguishable because of its uniform dark colouring. The male has conspicuously developed dorsal, caudal and anal fins. The transverse bars on the body are black at spawning time and the fins are red. The caudal fin is greatly extended by many loose thread-like fin rays. The fish is peaceable in captivity. It requires exclusively live food. At spawning time the males are pugnacious and quarrelsome with one another. Black Paradise-fish readily cross with the original form, the Paradise-fish (*M. opercularis opercularis*), and produce fertile progeny. The colour of the hybrids is dirty and unattractive.

218

219

Dwarf Croaking Gourami [220] (*Trichopsis pumilus*)

It is smaller than its 'croaking' relation (*T. vittatus*). It comes from southern Vietnam, Thailand and Sumatra and grows only to 3.5 cm long. The nest takes the form of a small foam ball (it may sometimes be discoid) which is attached to the underside of a broad leaf, or made in a flower pot or coconut shell close to the bottom (10–15 cm above the water bed). The brood number is small, being up to 350 in the best fed specimens. The fry hatch at water temperatures of 27–28°C within about 36 hours. Many pairs spawn several times in succession, in short intervals of four to seven days. The Dwarf Croaking Gourami is one of the species in which the males croak during courting. The free swimming fry are large enough to be able to swallow brine shrimp nauplii from the start.

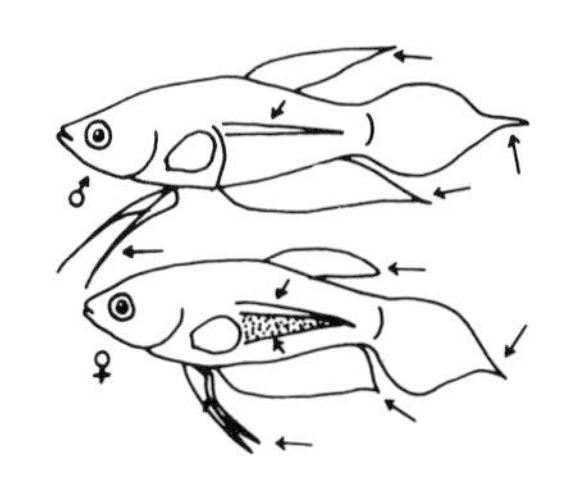

Trichopsis pumilus

220

Schaller's Gourami (*T. schalleri*) [221], which was found in Thailand and described in 1962 by Ladiges, has a similar appearance and the same breeding requirements.

221

Sharp-nosed Perch or **Marbled Climbing Perch** [222] (*Ctenopoma oxyrhynchus*)

This labyrinth fish is a native of the tributaries of the lower Congo. It grows up to 10 cm in length. It is quarrelsome, like other species of the genus *Ctenopoma*, and is not suitable for community tanks. It needs planty of vegetable food but greedily devours small fish as well. The breeding pairs spawn at depth in water at a temperature of 28 to 30°C. They do not build a foam nest. The eggs, containing a high proportion of fat, float on the surface. The fry retain their juvenile colour for some time; the posterior part of the body remains black.

About 2,000 young are produced at each spawning. From the beginning of free swimming they require tiny food, ideally rotifers and small nauplii of *Cyclops*. The young are light-shy. The fully developed male of the Sharp-nosed Perch is distinguished from the female by its longer dorsal and anal fins. The female's fins are more rounded, and its body is more thickset.

222

Chapter 8 CURIOUS FRESHWATER FISHES

This group of African **Freshwater Needles** [223] (*Syngnathus pulchellus*) is formed by males, females and the young. Impressing and 'pregnant' males have an abdomen of a purple-red colour; many of them have a brood pouch formed by two folds (bearing cavity) at the beginning of the lower side of the tail, of the same length as the abdomen itself, and full of progeny.

The fish described in this chapter are kept in freshwater aquariums all over the world. They come from every continent and represent 7 families but form just a fraction of the wide variety of species in these families. This means that it is difficult to list any common characteristics. The different species have found different ways of adapting to their natural environment and have developed interesting habits and modes of living. They may hatch their eggs in their mouths (although they are unrelated to cichlids); some of them leap over the water surface and glide on their broad pectoral fins, some shoot down flying insects with a drop of water. Others produce weak electric discharges for orientation and for marking their territory; and some live a secretive life, remaining buried in the substrate, while others crawl and skip in the half-dried mud of river banks, hunting insects.

Boeseman's Rainbowfish [224] (*Melanotaenia boesemani*)

Living in Lake Ajamara in the province of Irian Jaya in New Guinea, it belongs to the family Melanotaeniidae. The male is larger and more colourful than the female and grows up to 10 cm in length. At spawning time the eggs are deposited almost daily over the fine-leaved plants. Eggs are small (1.2 mm), their membrane has a cluster of long filaments by which they can be strongly fixed to the spawning substrate. At a water temperature of 26–27°C the embryo develops in the egg membrane for six and half days. The young are hatched, with full swimbladder, at night. At first they must be fed on small infusoria of the genus *Paramecium* or tiny rotifers (Rotatoria). After some three days they feed on freshly hatched nauplii of the brine shrimps *(Artemia salina)*. They grow slowly.

223 224

Arowana [225] (*Osteoglossum bicirrhosum*)

This fish inhabits the waters of Guyana and the Amazon basin. It grows to a length of 120 cm. Its dorsal and anal fins are long and are opposite each other. The fish of this species like to associate in shoals in stagnant and shallow waters in old river arms or in lakes. Their diet is extremely varied; they feed on any live food, from plankton to fish. The female keeps the eggs in her mouth until the young emerge. The smallest specimens greedily devour *Daphnia* and the larvae of gnats and many other water insects. When older, they prefer fish. Vegetable food may be added to their diet. Medium-size specimens make beautiful exhibits for public aquariums. It is advisable to keep the tank well covered as this species is a good leaper.

Primitive features are characteristic of the family Osteoglossidae. Fish of this family are close relatives of species of the family Arapaimidae, which includes the largest freshwater fish currently known – the South American *Arapaima gigas* which grows as much as 2 to 4.5 metres in length.

225

Butterfly-fish [226] (*Pantodon buchholzi*)

This belongs to the family Pantodontidae and comes from West Africa, the Congo and Niger basins and Cameroon. The adult specimens grow to 10–15 cm long. This fish lives near the surface where it is able to glide on its wide pectoral fins for a distance of 2 metres. Its pectoral fins often make flapping movements, resembling active flight.

226

Its prey consists of insects living near the water. In the aquarium it should be given cockroaches, crickets, large flies, insect larvae and small fish. Soft water with peat extract and temperatures between 25 and 30°C are recommended for breeding. During spawning the fish twist themselves around each other. The eggs are probably fertilized internally. They float on the water surface and the parents do not take care of them. The fry hatch within about three days. Breeding and rearing are difficult and success is never guaranteed.

227

African Knife-fish [227] (*Xenomystus nigri*)

This representative of the family of African knife-fishes (Notopteridae) is widely distributed from the estuary of the Nile to Liberia. The maximum length of adult specimens is 20 cm. The fish produces barking sounds by letting gas pass from the swimbladder to the digestive tract. The African Knife-fishes are peaceable inhabitants of the weedy reaches of great rivers and stagnant backwaters in Africa (close relatives are found in southern Asia). Their swimbladder functions as an additional respiratory organ. At night they seek food on the bottom. They feed on insect larvae, worms, snails and small fish. Water for these fish should be soft and rather warm (25 to 28°C). The brood is deposited on the water bed, on a stone, a piece of wood or in a pit in the sand. The eggs are guarded by one of the parents, usually the male. Young fish are suitable for the domestic aquarium. Adult specimens make interesting exhibits in public aquariums.

Spiny Eel [228] (*Macrognathus aculeatus*)

Distributed from India to the Malay Peninsula and the Moluccas (Indonesia), it lives in fresh and brackish waters and grows to a length of 35 cm. The females are larger than the males. In the aquarium it reaches sexual maturity when 12–15 cm long. In contrast to some related species its dorsal, caudal and anal fins are distinctly separate from each other. The fish hide during the day with their bodies buried in sand. Only in the evening and at night do they leave their hiding place. All suitably sized animals which can pass through their small mouths are devoured by this species. The tank should be planted with robust aquatic vegetation and stones, with pieces of wood on the bottom. The water should be medium-hard and preferably slightly salted with kitchen or sea salt. Partial water replacement from time to time and good filtration are beneficial to these fish. *Macrognathus aculeatus* is peaceable and tolerant of other species and can be kept together with other placid fish. It belongs to the family of spiny eels (Mastacembelidae).

228

Bedotia geayi [229]

This fish lives in freshwaters of Madagascar and grows to a length of about 15 cm in the wild and 7–8 cm in captivity. It is a placid fish and is happy in small aquariums. The male has a red margin around the caudal fin, whereas the margin of the female's caudal fin is translucent or milk-white. The breeding pairs spawn for several days in succession. The daily egg yield in the spawning season is very small. Each egg is provided with a thin filament and is suspended from an aquatic plant. The parents do not usually care for their eggs or fry. The free swimming young are big and greedily devour the nauplii of brine shrimp or *Cyclops*. Hard water, at least 10° dGH, is advisable for breeding this species. It belongs to the family Melanotaeniidae.

229

Dwarf Rainbowfish or **Black-lined Rainbowfish** [230]

Melanotaenia maccullochi

(*Melanotaenia maccullochi*)

This is perhaps the most popular aquarium fish of the family Atherinidae. In the wild it inhabits freshwaters of Queensland (Australia) in the vicinity of Cairns. The adult specimens are about 7 cm long. In the aquarium it is undemanding and feeds on any live food and is even content with dry and artificial food. Breeding is similar to that with the previous species. *Melanotaenia maccullochi* spawns in a single day. The fry hatch with-

230

in seven to ten days at 25°C. One spawning yields up to 200 young. Only freshwater species of the Atherinidae are kept in aquariums, although most representatives of this family are sea fish. Recently some of the freshwater atherinids have been reclassified as an independent family, the Melanotaeniidae.

Three-spined Stickleback [231] (*Gasterosteus aculeatus*)

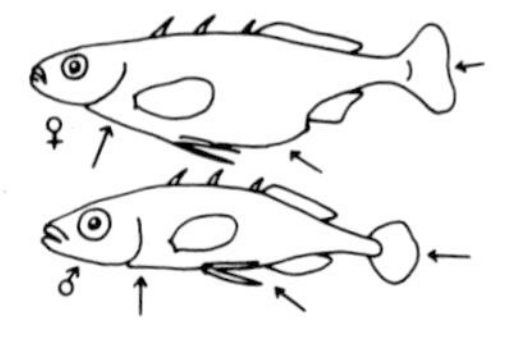

Gasterosteus aculeatus

The native waters of this fish are along European coasts, in north-eastern Asia, Algeria, and North America. It grows to about 10 cm long and prefers to live in brackish water. The number of free spines before the dorsal fin and bony plates on the flanks vary with the salinity of the water. At spawning time the male builds a nest from plant material on the bottom, where he spawns with several females in succession. The brood number is 90 to 250 eggs. The young hatch within 10–14 days and the male undertakes brood care.

In the aquarium the Three-spined Stickleback should be overwintered at low temperatures if possible. The summer temperature should also be low (22°C at most). Live food such as zooplankton, worms and larvae of chironomid midges should be provided. In its natural habitat it also eats fish fry. The male guards the progeny very energetically, even attacking feet in the wild or hands in the aquarium if they get close to the nest or shoal of young.

The stickleback family (Gasterosteidae) comprises five genera. Three of them represent marine dwellers and two live in fresh water. They are too small to be of any real commercial importance, but in some places (e.g. in Finland) people feed them to poultry.

232

Knight Goby [232] (*Stigmatogobius sadanundio*)

One of the few freshwater representatives of the gobies (Gobiidae). It is distributed in southern Asia, the Greater Sunda Islands (Indonesia) and the Philippines. It grows to 8 cm long. All gobies have fused pelvic fins, forming a basin-shaped sucker which enables the fish to attach themselves to a firm substrate. Almost all the fish of this family deposit their eggs on stones, with a special preference for crevices. The eggs adhere very firmly to the substrate. The males guard the eggs and young. Sea salt should be added to the water, the concentration depending on the origin of the fish. Gobies feed on plankton, the larvae of chironomid midges, fish meat, lamellibranches and algae. Large species are voracious eaters.

Chapter 9

BEAUTIES OF THE SOUTHERN SEAS

Lyretail Grouper [233] (*Variola louti*) attempts to frighten away an intruder.

Aquarium culture of sea fish is a relatively new branch in the world of aquaristics. Of marine organisms, invertebrates are more easily kept than fish. The main problem of keeping sea fish is their reluctance to reproduce in captivity; if they do reproduce, the young are very seldom reared. The other problems of marine aquaristics are the difficulties associated with growing sea plants (consumers of nitrogen compounds accumulating in the tank), the difficulty of providing suitable food substitutes for the fish since many species require a specific kind of food in nature, and the need for maintaining water purity. The water needs regular replacement with preparations of salt mixtures. Marine aquariums usually depend on continued imports of most species.

This last, brief chapter is not intended to give the reader a complete picture of the splendour and inexhaustible variety of the colour and form of sea fish. The aim is to use several examples to direct the reader's attention to the interesting aspects of those species which can be captured by the aquarium fish keeper in his travels. In this way the aquarist can avoid the great costs of expensive coral fish and the disappointment of possible failure to keep them alive. Apart from the delight of sea fishing the aquarist can learn about the natural habitats of the fish and employ this experience in preparing the aquarium so as to give the fish a chance to prosper. The species described in this chapter belong to various families and orders which will be briefly mentioned in the description of each species, since no general characteristics can be given.

Lyretail Grouper or **Painted Coral Bass** or **Fairy Cod** [233, 234] (*Variola louti*)

This belongs to the family Serranidae and is widespread in the Pacific Ocean and the Indian Ocean as far as South Africa and the Red Sea. It grows to a length of 130 cm and

◀ 233

is a very good marketable fish. It is of extremely variable ground colouring, from almost black through bluish-grey, orange, brown to shining red. The specimens of lighter colours have irregular dark spots in the upper half of the body. The whole body is covered with small white-blue luminous spots (violet in those living in the Red Sea). The hind part of all fins of young fish is yellow, which turns bluish in older individuals. The caudal fin is typically half-moon shaped. They like to hide in rocky and coral caves and are preyed on by other fishes. The Lyretail Grouper is a decorative addition to any large public aquarium. The average private fish keeper, however, can rear only very young specimens and these will soon outgrow his aquarium.

Brown Gaper [235] (*Serranellus hepatus*)

This common species of the Mediterranean Sea and the Atlantic grows to a length of about 15 cm. It is a small representative of the family Serranidae and inhabits rocky and sandy coastal waters as well as sea meadows with beds of aquatic plants of the genus *Zostera*. It is most frequently encountered in waters deeper than 10 metres. In summer it can be seen very close to the shore, 2–3 meters below the water surface. It is a hermaphroditic species; the glands of both sexes developing simultaneously in each fish. Hence each fish is capable of fertilizing itself. Its spawning time is June and July. It is very suitable for domestic aquariums and is undemanding, slow and very inquisitive. It devours water crustaceans, the meat of swan mussels, lean poultry meat and so on. It should be fed moderately since it is very voracious.

235

236

Green-eyed Wrasse [236] (*Crenilabrus ocellatus*)

An inhabitant of quays and of beds of the plants *Cystoseira* and *Zostera*, it lives in the coastal waters of the Mediterranean and Adriatic seas and in the Atlantic, at depths from 0.5 metres. The male grows to 12 cm long; the female only 6 cm. During the spawning season from May to August, the male gradually builds several nests from the fine filaments of algae, particularly of the genus *Cladophora*. However, if this is not available, almost any other red, green or brown seaweed will serve just as well. The dish-shaped nest is the size of a plate and is built on the bottom. Young males up to the size of 7–9 cm do not build nests. Females with ripe eggs wander along the coast in shoals and spawn in the nests with both large and small males. If rival males meet they take up a frontal posture and rapidly raise their gill covers, which are brilliantly coloured in the design of a peacock's eye. The larger males fan the eggs and fry in the nest by moving the pectoral fins while adopting an oblique position with the head down. This species is suitable for the domestic aquarium. The water in the tank must be clean and well aerated. The fish needs both meat and vegetable food.

The **Mediterranean Wrasse** (*Crenilabrus mediterraneus*, family Labridae) lives along the coast of the Mediterranean Sea and also in the Atlantic Ocean near Portugal, the Azores and the western coast of Africa. The male is larger, growing to 17 cm long, and is splendidly dark red or bluish. In May to June the pair builds a simple nest from a clump of algae at the border between the rocky and sandy bottom. The male spits sand into the nest; then the female deposits the eggs. The males are very aggressive and vigorously guard their residence. The fish of this species are very hardy in the aquarium. As they are voracious they demand a varied diet of meat.

Five-spot Wrasse [237] (*Crenilabrus quinquemaculatus*)

This fish is widely distributed in the intertidal zone of the Mediterranean and Adriatic seas. It often seeks refuge in rock crevices and in the stands of seaweed of the genus *Cystoseira*. It grows up to 16 cm long.

The spawning season extends from April to June. The fish make a nest in the bottom sand or in a rock depression. The nest is provided with a large crescent-shaped front wall reinforced with red, green or brown algae or with small stones. The males stay at the same site for up to a year. The aquarium must be provided with plenty of hiding places among stones. The picture 237 shows a female.

Its relative, the **Ashy Wrasse** (*Crenilabrus cinereus*), is a delicate species which is found in the Adriatic and Mediterranean seas and in coastal waters of the Atlantic. It does not grow larger than 11 cm in length. The fish keep close to stands of sea plants such as *Zostera* and *Posidonia*. They spawn in May and June, in shallow waters at a depth of 50–70 cm. They make a furrow about as long as their body in the sand and reinforce its front wall with seaweed of the genus *Cladophora* and spat sand. They lie on the brood with their heads turned up and bravely drive away all intruders, however large they may be.

237

238

Doederlein's Wrasse [238] (*Crenilabrus doederleini*)

This smallest species of the genus *Crenilabrus* is found in the Mediterranean and Adriatic seas but nowhere is it common. It grows only 10 cm long. It lives mainly among vegetation, especially in meadows of sea-grass (*Zostera marina*). The male is red or orange with a broad brown longitudinal band on the flanks with a silver band underneath. The females are green [238]. It is the least voracious species of the genus *Crenilabrus*. It is shy and likes to hide in the stands of plants or in narrow cracks in rocks.

The **Black-tail Wrasse** (*Symphodus melanocerus*) lives in the Mediterranean and Adriatic seas. It prefers the densely vegetated littoral zone, where it occurs in large populations. Quays are also a favoured habitat. It has an elongated body which grows up to 14 cm long. Young specimens are perhaps the only real 'cleaners' in the seas where they live. They remove the dermal parasites from other wrasses (Labridae) as well as from groupers (Serranidae) and porgies or sea breams (Sparidae). The fish that wishes to be cleaned usually takes up an unusual vertical, head-up position, signalling its readiness for cleaning. However, *Symphodus melanocerus* does not live only on parasites. In the aquarium it will take the meat of molluscs, shellfish, crayfish and pieces of fish or even lean poultry meat.

239

Bluehead [239, 240] (*Thalassoma bifasciatum*)

This fish of the Caribbean Sea and the waters around Bermuda, southern Florida and the southern part of the Gulf of Mexico grows to a length of about 14 cm. The youngest specimens are either whitish or yellow, with a black longitudinal band on the flanks. The band disappears with age and the body colour of the fish changes to canary yellow. At this colour stage (at a length of about 4 cm) the fish are mature and the males and females take on the same colour [239]. Only the males then continue to grow and change colour. Their head becomes blue and the body green, with two transverse bars behind the pectoral fins [240]. Young Blueheads usually clean the skin of other fishes by removing parasites from them. They are attractive components of the aquarium, greedily taking food such as frozen brine shrimp and pieces of meat, as well as dried food of all kinds.

240

Four-blue-streak Cleanerfish [241] (*Labaricus quadrilineatus*)

This is a typical cleaner which is native to the Red Sea. It grows up to a length of about 12 cm. Its body is torpedo-shaped and most locomotory thrust is provided by the pectoral fins, giving the fish a characteristic swinging movement which probably signals that the fish is ready to offer a 'cleaning service'. The ground colour is blue-black with brilliant blue longitudinal bands. Like the **Blue Streak** (*Labroides dimidiatus*), the fish of this species run a 'cleaning shop' in certain places among coral cliffs. They are visited by sick fish at certain hours of the day, which patiently queue for their turn.

241

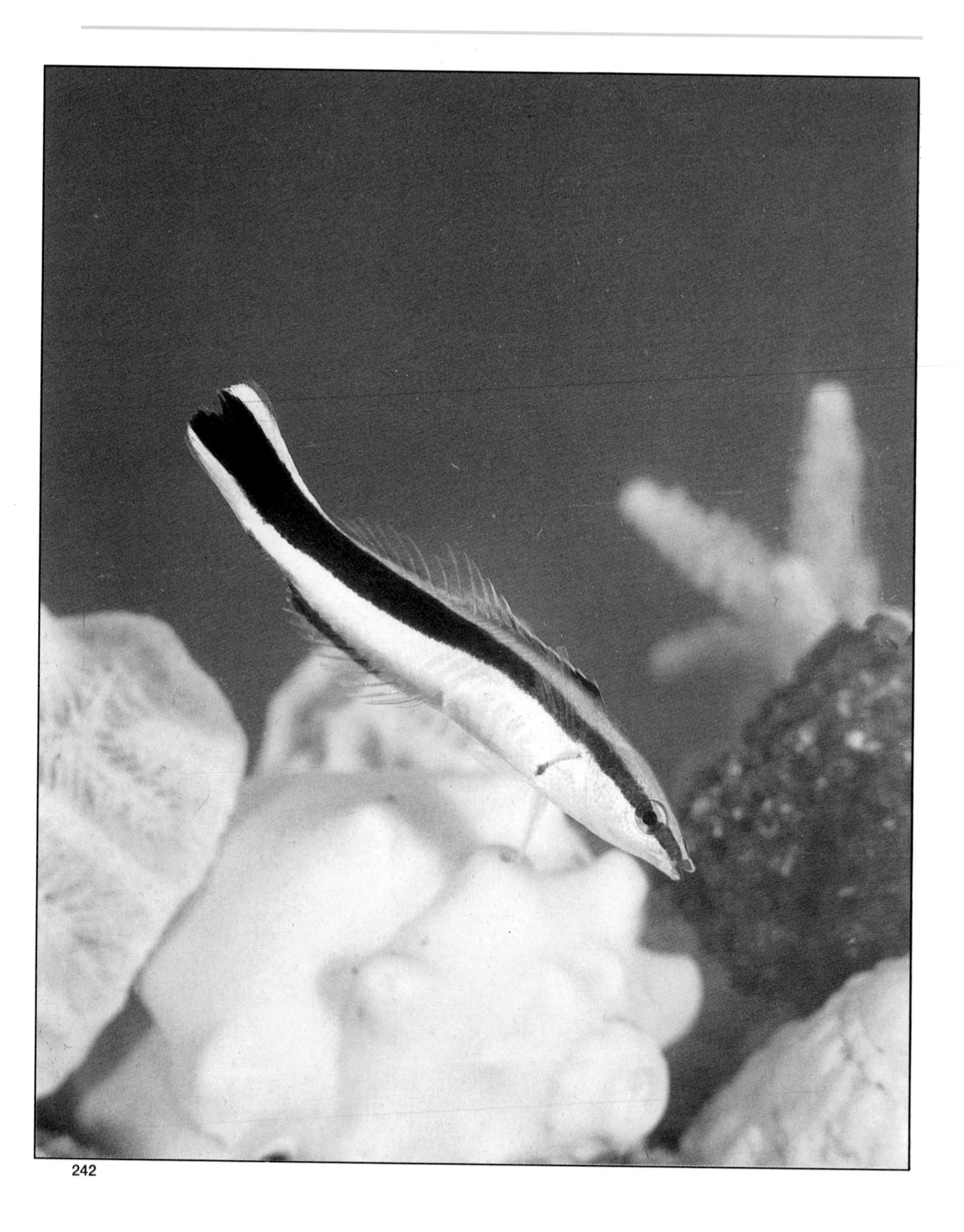

242

Labroides dimidiatus [242] and *Labaricus quadrilineatus*, like other cleaner wrasses, clean the body surface of other fish, but also pick parasites from the mouths and gills through the raised gill covers of larger fish. The parasites of larger fish form a major part of the diet of these two species, which can therefore be successfully kept in aquariums only together with large fish species.

Blue-grey Wrasse [243] (*Coris formosa*)

Also belonging to the family Labridae, this is a common fish of the Indian and Pacific oceans. The young individuals differ in colour from the adults. The ground colour of a young *C. formosa* is almost the same as that of the related *C. gaimard*. In both, a red to brown colour prevails and is interrupted by transverse and wedge-shaped white spots surrounded by a darker shade. The adult specimens of both species are up to 40 cm long. In adult *C. formosa* the ground colour is grey-blue with small black spots; the throat is violet and the part of the head in front of the broad, oblique, blue-white band under the eye is yellow to orange. The end of the caudal fin and the margin of the anal fin are bluish.

Both species can be kept in the aquarium for a long time without much difficulty. They need a sandy bottom in which they can bury themselves for the night. Individuals should be kept separately since the adolescent fish are quarrelsome. The diet should vary, with a prevalence of live food. The fish do not do well if fed permanently on dry or frozen food or food substitutes.

243

Rainbow Wrasse [244] (*Coris julis*)

The Rainbow Wrasse can be found in the eastern Atlantic from Great Britain to the Gulf of Guinea and in the Mediterranean and Adriatic seas. Formerly ichthyologists recognized two species, *C. julis* and *C. giofredi*. However, it was later found that the latter's colouring is typical of the immature stage, particularly among the females, of *C. julis*. After a short transitional period [244] they change their coloration and resemble the beautifully coloured males. The male grows to a length of 25 cm. It has an orange longitudinal stripe on the flanks. The back is usually blue-green and the front part of the body has blue stripes. The ground colour of the females is brown or olive-brown with one yellow and two dark blue, red or black stripes on the flanks. It is interesting that the males are sexually most active in the transition between the female to male colour phase. As soon as they have taken on the beautiful colouring of the male, they fall into a sort of sexual senility. The colour of the Rainbow Wrasse is variegated. It keeps swimming throughout the day but buries itself in sand at night. The fish move to deeper waters in winter. In spring they return to the coastal waters where they spawn. The small eggs, 0.65 mm in diameter, float on a large round drop of oil. In the aquarium the Rainbow Wrasse cannot withstand excessively high temperatures; it prospers in water at 21–23°C. Individuals of this species are voracious and eat any meat, particularly freshwater molluscs, brine shrimps or pieces of fish meat. They are easily fed in the aquarium, where they thrive and may live for a long time.

244

245

Fairy Basslet or **Royal Gramma** [245] (*Gramma hemichrysos*)

This species of the family Serranidae is common in the Caribbean Sea. It only grows to a length of 6 cm. In the wild it lives among coral cliffs at depths of 4–6 metres. Whether it is kept alone or in a shoal, it always needs plenty of hiding places in the aquarium. Like the large groupers, it likes to stand guard in front of its 'home'. Each specimen inhabits a territory which it aggressively defends against other fish of its own kind. The water should be crystal clear and very warm, about 28°C. This fish is not very choosy about its food and can be given dry food for a short time. It is difficult to catch and therefore the supply to aquarists is limited.

Yellowhead Wrasse [246] (*Halichoeres garnoti*)

This fish is widespread in the Caribbean Sea and in the south-western Atlantic Ocean. It is found in the waters around the Bahamas and near mainland coasts from Florida to south-eastern Brazil. It lives near cliffs at a depth of 50 metres. The young resemble the species *H. maculipinna*, but the black lengthwise strip is lower on the sides of their body. The males usually grow to 14 cm, the females are smaller. The largest individuals grow to 19 cm.

246

247

Mediterranean Bluehead Wrasse [247] (*Thalassoma pavo*)

This species is native to the waters of the eastern Atlantic Ocean and the Mediterranean Sea. It grows to some 20 cm and is of various colours depending on its age and area of origin. The individuals from the Mediterranean Sea are brownish, while in those from the Desertas Islands (Madeira) a basic green colouring is dominant [247]. They thrive in a water temperature of 21 to 24°C. They can live for a long time, but they are aggressive not only towards others of their species, but also to other fish in the tank.

Sabre Squirrelfish [248] (*Sargocentron spiniferum*)

This belongs to the family of soldier fishes (Holocentridae). The species is abundant from the central part of the Pacific (Oceania, the Hawaiian Islands) westwards through the Indian Ocean to South Africa. The colour picture shows fish from the Red Sea. It grows to 36 cm. Other fish of the same species have lengthwise bands. This one is of compact bright red colour; the pectoral and pelvic fins and the rear part of the dorsal and anal fins are bright yellow. It has a conspicuously big yellowish to bluish 'thorn' on the rear lower side of the fore gillcover. Only the young are suitable for aquariums owing to the adults' aggressiveness and size. They like every kind of meat.

Banded Butterfly Fish [249] (*Chaetodon striatus*)

This fish is widespread in the western Atlantic from Brazil through Bermudan waters and northwards to Massachusetts and grows to a maximum length of 15 cm. It lives near reefs, but can also be seen during the ebb-tide in pools with sea-grass plants.

248

Striking crosswise and soft lengthwise bands form perfect protective colouring, and it easily escapes the attention of diving birds. It feeds greedily and is a long liver. Unfortunately, it is hard to fish and therefore imported into Europe only rarely.

249

250

251

Long-nosed Butterfly Fish [250] (*Chelmon rostratus*)

This coral fish of the family Chaetodontidae is widespread in the Indopacific region. It grows to a length of about 17 cm. Success or failure to acclimatize this species always depends on the food. The fish has narrow protruding jaws and with these it picks food from the crevices of coral reefs. Plankton floating on the water surface is usually refused, but small pieces of mollusc or fish attached to the sharp twigs of corals may be offered. It will follow other fish which pick their food from the bottom. This peaceable fish is particularly fond of swimming among branches of corals.

Half-masked Butterfly Fish [251] (*Chaetodon semilarvatus*)

This fish inhabits the Red Sea, where it grows to about 20 cm. It is a delightful and popular species for sea aquariums, but it is rarely imported. The most important thing is to acclimatize the fish to dried or frozen foods as soon as possible. Only such acclimatized specimens become tame and long-living inhabitants of the aquarium.

Flag or **Threadfin Butterfly Fish** [252] (*Chaetodon auriga*)

This lives in the Pacific and Indian oceans and in the Red Sea. Individuals from the coastal waters of Australia grow up to 20 cm long while those from Hawaii are only 14 cm long. It is one of the hardiest marine aquarium species. Within a few hours in a tank they adapt to the new environment and begin to take food. They are not choosy; freeze-dried crustaceans are devoured as greedily as pieces of live food. The fish soon become very voracious and should regularly be given smaller but more frequent rations. Long starvation is as harmful as overfeeding.

252

Four-eyed Butterfly Fish [253] (*Chaetodon capistratus*)

This commonest species of the genus lives in the tropical parts of the Atlantic and in the Carribbean Sea. In the wild it likes to eat the tentacles of polychaete tubeworms and sea anemones. In captivity it should be possible to acclimatize it to other foods, preferably freeze-dried tubifex worms or brine shrimps, or even live worms. Unfortunately, some specimens do not adapt to the new food and die within eight to ten weeks. The fish is constantly supplied to the American market but less frequently imported into Europe.

253

Common Butterfly Fish [254] (*Parachaetodon ocellatus*)

Inhabiting the tropical part of the Indopacific, this species grows up to 15 cm long. It adapts to aquarium life quickly and willingly takes food. It is thermophilic and likes temperatures of 25–28°C. The food should consist of brine shrimps, enchytraeids, shrimps and molluscs. The fish stays in the lower layers of water, close to the water bed. It is placid and avoids flights. Unlike the related species, it soon loses its shyness.

Emperor Butterfly Fish [255] (*Chaetodontoplus mesoleucus*)

The Emperor Butterfly Fish lives in the coral reefs of the Red Sea and grows to a length of about 16 cm. Like all fish from this region, it is thermophilic and thrives in a temperature of 28°C. It is easy to keep and soon begins to take food such as pieces of various crustaceans (e.g. *Mysis* or shrimps) and molluscs. It enjoys tubifex worms. Unfortunately, it is often unsociable and tends to harass other fish in the tank.

254

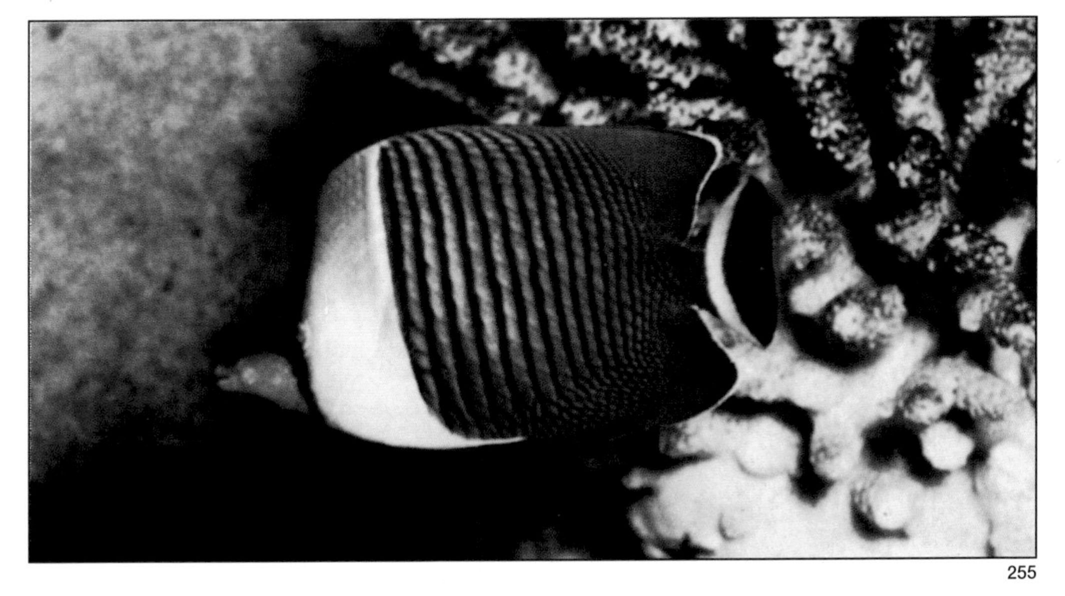

255

Poor Man's Moorish Idol [256] (*Heniochus acuminatus*)

Native to the Pacific and Indian oceans and the Red Sea, it reaches a maximum length of about 25 cm. Fish of the genus *Heniochus* associate in large shoals. They have conspicuous dark transverse bars and yellow pectoral, dorsal and caudal fins. Young specimens have 11 to 13 spinous rays in the dorsal fin, with the fourth ray being produced as a filamentous process. *Heniochus acuminatus* is very hardy and undemanding in the aquarium. It can be given practically any food and sometimes takes it directly from the hand. It is very susceptible to substances containing copper. It is a very popular marine aquarium fish.

256

257

Scat or **Argus-fish** [257] (*Scatophagus argus*)

This species of the family Scatophagidae inhabits the coastal waters of the Indopacific tropics. When fully grown it is about 30 cm long. It lives in sea, brackish and fresh water but the adult specimens thrive best in sea water. The generic name means excrement-eater and this is a reference to the fact that it often stays near sewage outlets. It is omnivorous and in the aquarium it will accept all kinds of live food, as well as algae, lettuce, spinach and soaked porridge oats. The mouth of this fish is small. It swims in a swaying style like the coral fish. Food is incompletely digested in its alimentary canal and, in consequence, its excrement pollutes the water and forms a large amount of detritus which must be removed from the aquarium by constant filtration of the water. A subspecies of the Scat, the Red Argus (*Scatophagus argus rubrifrons*), has a red forehead. Young specimens are spotted and have vertical stripes, whereas the adults are uniformly green or brown.

Two other species, *S. tetracanthus* and *Selenotoca multifasciata* (also of the family Scatophagidae), are imported from time to time. All require breeding temperatures between 20 and 28°C. The spawning habits are similar to those of the lithophilous cichlids. Young specimens retain a bony cuirass on the head and shoulders for a long time. All attempts to breed any of these fish in captivity have failed.

Clown Anemone Fish [258] (*Amphiprion ocellaris*)

The Clown Anemone Fish belongs to the anemone fish family Pomacentridae, comprising some 15 genera and almost 200 species. The genus *Amphiprion* itself contains 26 species. *Amphiprion ocellaris* is most widespread in the Indian Ocean and in the western parts of the Pacific. This beautifully coloured and popular fish grows up to 10 cm. It is not easy to keep in the aquarium. Like other anemone fish species, it lives exclusively with the large anemone species. They can often be seen swimming among the stinging tentacles of sea-anemones (*Discosoma* and *Stoichactis*). Like other fish, sea-anemone fish are not immune to anemone poison, but apparently the anemone does not discharge its protective nematocysts towards these fish. In times of danger the anemone fish find refuge among the twigs of corals. The Clown Anemone Fish and some other anemone fish have been successfully reproduced in captivity. The eggs are laid and cared for on the stems of sea-anemones, hidden under the stinging tentacles.

258

Red Clown [259] (*Amphiprion frenatus*)

Living in the Pacific and Atlantic oceans, it grows up to 14 cm long. Aquarists claim that it is the hardiest of the anemone fish species and is the least dependent on sea-anemones. It has been successfully bred in captivity. Picture 259 shows the female.

Gold-finned Clown [260] (*Amphiprion sebae*)

This fish occurs widely in the Pacific and Indian oceans and grows to 10 cm long. It is a close relative of the **Saddle Back Clown** (*A. polymnus*); the two species differ only slightly. In the Saddle Back Clown the second white band of the adult never reaches down to the belly but remains in the dorsal fin as a saddle-shaped patch and just

259

reaches to the middle dorsal part of the body. *A. sebae* is easily kept in aquariums, but it needs more care than *A. frenatus*.

The majority of the anemone fish are difficult to identify, since the colours of the young of many specimes are almost identical. This is why some reference works often give different names to the same fish. An excellent description of the genus *Amphiprion* was published in 1972 by G. R. Allen, who studied the different developmental stages of all known species in nature, identified them exactly, and documented his work with many photographs and drawings.

260

Yellow-tailed Anemone Fish [261] (*Amphiprion latifasciatus*)

Aquaristic literature usually refers to this species as *Amphiprion xanthurus*. It lives in the Indian Ocean. Fully grown specimens are up to 12 cm long. It is a hardy species in captivity. It swims among the stinging tentacles of sea-anemones and is not particular about the species of sea-anemone with which it lives.

261

White-tailed Damselfish [262] (*Dascyllus aruanus*)

This is a common fish of Indopacific waters and of the Red Sea. Particularly large shoals of this species live off the coasts of South Africa, India, Australia, China, and Melanesia. It grows to about 8 cm long.

D. aruanus is frequently confused with the **Black-tailed Humbug** (*D. melanurus*) which has a broad black blotch on the caudal fin. *D. aruanus* is a very popular aquarium fish and is imported in large numbers, mainly from the Philippines and Sri Lanka. It is easy to keep in the domestic aquarium, despite the fact that it tends to be aggressive. This and other species of the genus *Dascyllus* are particularly suitable for beginners to keep in sea aquariums.

262

Three-spot Damselfish [263] (*Dascyllus trimaculatus*)

Occurring mainly in the Red Sea, off South Africa and in Polynesia, this fish grows to 12 cm long. The adult individuals can easily be confused with the Hawaiian species *D. albisella*, which has a single, large white blotch in the middle of the body. The young can very easily be distinguished because, in addition to the blotch on the middle of the body, *D. trimaculatus* has another white spot on the front of the head. However, the blotches gradually disappear with age and the body colour of both species becomes uniformly dark. *D. trimaculatus* is a hardy species that feeds on small crustaceans which are picked out from the branches of corals among which they live. In its natural hab-

263

itat the food consists of small shrimps and crab larvae. The fish also pick parasites from the bodies of other fish. In aquariums they greedily accept freeze-dried brine shrimps.

264

Marginate Damselfish [264] (*Dascyllus marginatus*)

This fish is widely distributed in the Red Sea and probably also through the tropical latitudes of the Indopacific. It grows to 8 cm long. Care and breeding in the aquarium is simple and is much the same as with *Dascyllus trimaculatus*.

265

Neon Devil [265] (*Abudefduf oxyodon*)

The Indo-Australian region of the Pacific is the habitat of this species, which grows up to a length of 10 cm. It can be acclimatized to food replacers but the aquarist often faces other problems when keeping this species. Despite its small size it is very aggressive and is also susceptible to various diseases which can be fatal.

Blue Devil [266] (*Glyphidodontops cyaneus*)

Living in the southern parts of the Indo-Australian archipelago; it associates in shoals over coral reefs. The eggs are deposited on filamentous algae. The male guards the brood for three to four days. In the aquarium fish of this species readily accept live and dry food substitutes. They are often quarrelsome.

266

Orange-tailed Reef Fish [267] (*Glyphidodontops hemicyaneus*)

This is a native of the Indo-Australian regions and grows to a length of 6 cm. It is blue and its caudal peduncle and caudal fin are yellow. With increasing age the blue colour becomes darker and duller, but the bright orange colour of the caudal peduncle is retained. Life habits of *G. hemicyaneus* are the same as those of *G. cyaneus*.

267

268

Emperor Angelfish [268, 269] (*Pomacanthodes imperator*)

This species, which lives in the Indian Ocean especially around Madagascar, grows to 40 cm in length. This species belongs to the family Pomacanthidae. The members of this family differ from the butterfly-fish (Chaetodontidae) as they have a strong spine on the lower part of the gill cover. Some species stay in pairs while others prefer solitude. It is certainly the most splendidly coloured species of tropical seas. In many pomacanthid species the colours change several times throughout their life. They swim in a characteristic interrupted movement. The Emperor Angelfish finds its food on corals and stones. It often keeps close to small caves in which it hides from

269

danger. If disturbed it can produce clapping sounds which are clearly audible under water. All angelfish must be given vegetable supplements (preferably lettuce) to their regular food. Some of them are very sensitive and reluctant to accept food replacers.

The young of the Emperor Angelfish are deep blue with many concentric white rings on the body [269] and a complex pattern on the fins which changes with age. The colour keeps changing until the fish are mature. The adults [268] are reddish to purple and have 20 to 28 yellow horizontal stripes which run from the head to the base of the orange caudal fin. The Emperor Angelfish readily allows itself to be freed of parasites by the cleaner fish *Labroides dimidiatus*. In the aquarium it requires a water temperature of 25°C. It will readily accept replacer foods.

Ringed Emperor Angelfish or **Blue King Angelfish** [270]

(*Pomacanthodes annularis*)

This fish is widely distributed in the Pacific and Indian oceans, particularly off the coasts of Australia, India and Sri Lanka. In the neighbourhood of Sri Lanka it also inhabits turbid waters. In this area the young emerge in January, which is the warmest season of the year. At this time they can be captured easily. The adults are very hard to catch since they hide among corals during the day. Fishing is most likely to be successful on moonlit nights when the Ringed Emperor Angelfish rest on rocks as if asleep. They can be easily caught in small nets since they appear to be transfixed by the light from a lantern.

270

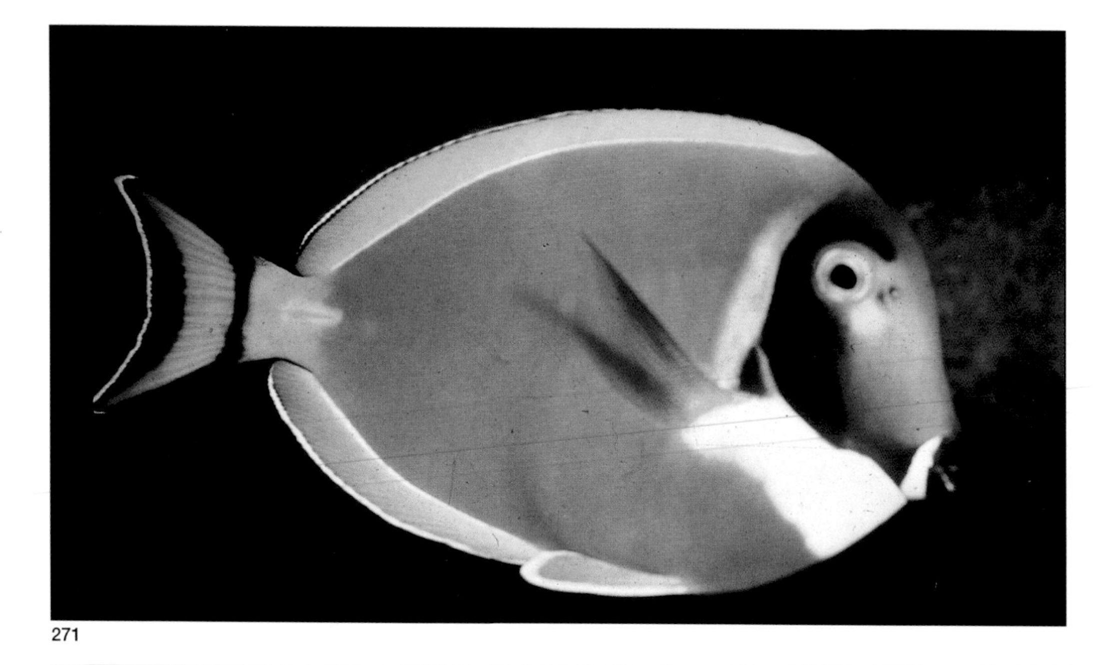
271

White-throated Surgeonfish [271] (*Acanthurus leucosternon*)

The Indian and Pacific oceans, especially the coastal waters of East Africa and the Comoro Islands, are the home of this species. Owing to its beautiful colours it is very popular among aquarists. It is an omnivorous species but vegetable food is preferred to animal food. It requires a rather high water temperature of 25–28°C.

272

Red-toothed Filefish [272] (*Odonus niger*)

This is a common species of the Indian and Pacific oceans and one of the most frequently kept aquarium species of all the triggerfishes (Balistidae). It is placid and tame and will accept meat from the hand. The teeth are orange to red.

Half-moon Angelfish [273] (*Arusetta asfur*)

Belonging to the family Pomacanthidae, this fish comes from the Red Sea and grows to a length of about 16 cm. It acclimatizes readily in the aquarium and can live for a long time. Supplementary vegetable food is eagerly accepted by this species.

273

Sharp-nosed Puffer or **Ocellated Toby** [274] (*Canthigaster solandri*)

This common species of the Pacific and Indian oceans and the Red Sea belongs to the family of tobies (Canthigasteridae). Its eyes move independently of one another. The fish of this species are extremely inquisitive. Like all tobies and the puffer-fishes, to which they are closely related, they eat snails and any live or dead meat they happen to find in the aquarium. In this way they keep the water of the aquarium clean and free from pollution. Frozen and dried food, such as brine shrimps and tubifex worms, is also accepted.

274

Black-spotted Puffer [275] (*Arothron nigropunctatus*)

This inhabitant of the Indian and Pacific oceans can be found from South Africa to Polynesia. Around the Seychelles it grows to 35 cm long, while those caught farther to the east are probably somewhat smaller. It is remarkable in the aquarium for its lemon yellow colour with irregularly distributed tiny black dots. Its teeth are white. It likes to feed on live corals and accepts food replacers with reluctance.

White-spotted Blowfish [276] (*Arothron hispidus*)

A native of the waters around the Seychelles and many other regions of the Indian and Pacific oceans, it grows to about 50 cm long. At the base of the pectoral fins and gill openings (clefts) the fish bears a yellow ovoid pattern with a pale ring-like rim. The body colours of the young are more pronounced than those of the adults. Their favourite food consists of marine crustaceans. In captivity they will also take molluscs and other animal food. They like to hide in corals or under stones.

275

276

Speckled Angelfish [277] (*Pomacanthodes maculosus*)

The Speckled Angelfish belongs to the family Pomacanthidae. It is native to the Red Sea and grows to a length of 40 cm. The distinctive feature of the species is a transverse, crescent design in the middle of its body. It acclimatizes easily in the aquarium and remains in good condition for a long time. The food should contain vegetable supplements. Aquarists sometimes confuse it with *Arusetta asfur* (see page 233).

277

Black Angelfish [278] (*Pomacanthus arcuatus*)

The Black Angelfish comes from the Caribbean Sea and grows to a length of 40 cm. As with all species of the family Pomacanthidae, the young individuals have different colouring from the adults. While the young specimens are dark to black, with light transverse stripes, the adult fish are grey with dark skirted rims to the fins and with a black spot on each scale. The dorsal and anal fins are enormously developed and strongly elongate in the hind part. The young are very similar to the young of the species *Pomacanthus paru*. In the aquarium they are not finicky feeders and will eat live, frozen and artificial food. However, they are very sensitive to impurities in the water and are very vulnerable to fungal infections.

Fight Firefish [279] (*Pterois miles*)

This fish is closely related, if not identical, to the **Red Firefish** (*Pterois volitans*), which lives in the Red Sea, near South Africa and around Polynesia. It grows to a length of

278

25–35 cm. Its body is covered with wide alternating dark and light transverse bands. The membranes in the dorsal fin and in the pectoral fins develop into fan-like projections.

279

280

Snakehead Goby [280] (*Gobius ophiocephalus*)

This belongs to the family of gobies (Gobiidae), whose pelvic fins are fused, or at least partially fused, to form a sucking disc. The family includes many small tropical species which live in the surf zone. *Gobius ophiocephalus* occurs mainly in the Mediterranean and Adriatic seas. It grows up to 10 cm long. It likes to live among *Zostera* beds. Adults spawn from March to May. The species adapts easily to aquarium conditions and greedily takes various animal foods.

Bucchichi's Goby or **Striped Goby** [281] (*Gobius bucchichii*)

Occurring in the surf zone of the Mediterranean and Adriatic seas, this goby is also frequently found in harbours. The fish always keeps close to the sea-anemone *Anemonia sulcata*. The mucus film on their bodies protects them against the stinging tentacles of *Anemonia sulcata*, but not against those of other sea-anemone species. The fish is not completely dependent on the anemones; it only seeks refuge among their tentacles when in danger. Crustaceans and pieces of meat are the best food for this species.

Tentacle Blenny [282] (*Parablennius tentacularis*)

The Tentacle Blenny belongs to the family of the blennies (Blenniidae), which live in the coastal zones of all temperate and tropical seas. Some species also live in brackish

281

waters, while others are found in freshwaters. A revision of the tribe Blenniini was published in 1977 by H. Bath. According to this work, the tribe has 15 genera and 70 species.

Parablennius tentacularis occurs commonly in the Mediterranean and Adriatic seas where it lives in stone crevices and among rocks overgrown with plants of the genus *Posidonia*. In their natural habitat the males form and defend their own territories and take care of the brood. In the aquarium this fish must have plenty of hiding places, some of which can be chosen by the male and protected against all rivals. If there is a shortage of hiding places the males soon kill one another. *Parablennius tentacularis* grows to a length of about 15 cm.

282

Dark-striped Blenny [283] (*Parablennius rouxi*)

The Dark-striped Blenny (*Parablennius rouxi*) inhabits the rocky coastal waters of the Adriatic and Mediterranean seas. It stays on rounded stones in water which reaches a depth of about 25 metres. In recent years large shoals of this fish have been observed close to the outlets of city sewage canals from the town of Komiža, on the island of Vis. *Parablennius rouxi* grows to 7 cm long. The male is larger and more robust than the female. On the front part of the dorsal fin the male has a brilliant blue oval 'mirror' and the tentacles above the eyes are larger than the female's. In the aquarium this fish needs special care; the water should be rich in oxygen and the temperature should be kept low.

An even smaller fish of this family, the **Adrian Blenny** *(Lipophrys adriaticus)*, is a native of the Adriatic and Mediterranean seas. It seeks refuge in the holes left by the burrowing bivalve *Pholas dactylus* at the low-tide mark. Individuals of this species do not grow longer than 5 cm. The males stay in the holes with only their heads sticking out while protecting the brood. They leave the hiding place to seek food in early morning and late evening when the tide is high.

Another very small representative of the family is the **Dalmatian Blenny** (*Lipophrys dalmatinus*), which grows only to 4 cm long. Habits and distribution are the same as in *L. adriaticus*. The heads of the males are bright yellow and may be seen sticking out of holes. The aquarium in which this species is to be kept can be small but must have narrow hiding places. The fish eats crustaceans, worms and pieces of molluscs.

283

284

Bloodthirsty Blenny [284] (*Pictiblennius sanguinolentus*)

This common fish of the Black, Adriatic and Mediterranean seas and the Atlantic Ocean grows to about 20 cm long. It differs from other blennies by swimming freely close to the bottom. It is very shy and often changes its hiding place. Spawning time is from April to August. The male protects a large brood (3,000–12,000 eggs) under a stone or in a crack among stones. Its ground colour is olive green, yellowish or sometimes brown, depending mainly on the colour of the substrate on which the fish lives. The rims of the pectoral fins bear red spots. Another species, the **Tompot Blenny** (*Parablennius gattorugine*), is still larger (20–25 cm long) and has huge tentacles branched like a tree. The meat of all blennies is tasty and highly regarded in some countries.

Zvonimir's Blenny (*Pictiblennius zvonimiri*) occurs in abundance in the rocky coastal waters of the Black, Mediterranean and Adriatic seas where it lives in narrow crevices among stones and rocks, usually on the shaded sides of islands. The male is larger than the female and grows to a length of about 7 cm. His head is brown-red in colour. At spawning time he entices the female by swaying movements; then he leads her to his cave, while bending his body up and down. Fish of this species acclimatize easily in the aquarium. The main requirement is water purity.

The **Capuchin Blenny** (*Coryphoblennius gaterita*) is found in the waters of the North African coast of the Mediterranean Sea, in the Atantic Ocean and in the English Channel up to the North Sea. It lives in fissures and cracks in rocks or under stones. It rides the surf and often jumps onto land, where it seeks food such as *Chthamalus stellatus*. It grows to 7 cm. The water in its aquarium must be rich in oxygen.

Cat's Blenny [285] (*Lipophrys canevae*)

This fish can be found sporadically in the waters along the Adriatic and Mediterranean coasts and usually keeps in groups below low-tide level. It grows to 7 cm long. At spawning time, which extends from June to August, the fighting males are splendidly coloured. A male in spawning livery shows gill covers which are shining yellow to orange-red, has a blue to black forehead and dark grey cheeks. When they attack one another, they arch their backs. In courtship displays they raise the gill covers and when luring the female they jerk their heads and swim a zig-zag course to show the female the way.

285

Sphinx Blenny [287] (*Aidablennius sphynx*)

Living in the Black, Adriatic and Mediterranean seas, this fish grows to 8 cm long. It is a splendid multi-coloured fish with a high dorsal fin. Spawning time is May and June and the eggs are laid in small caves. The male removes all sand, algae, shells and so on, and carries this material in its mouth far away from the spawning place. The Sphinx Blenny always stays in the intertidal zone and does not leave the brood (provided it does not dry out), even at low tide, or it returns immediately with the high tide. It has a very good sense of orientation; if removed 50 metres away from the nest, it finds it again within 24 hours. It adapts easily to aquarium conditions; it is very inquisitive and its favourite food consists of planktonic crustaceans as well as tubifex worms and small pieces of beef and lean poultry meat.

286

Eyed Blenny [286] (*Salaria pavo*)

The Eyed Blenny is abundant in the Black, Adriatic and Mediterranean seas. It grows to about 12 cm long. The male has a huge helmet-like hump on the head. The fish lives in hollows under stones. The eggs are deposited in crevices in rocks and are protected by the males. The eggs are never left, even during low tide. This species is easily kept in the aquarium. It is important to provide plenty of hiding places for individual males. If the tank is small or if there are not enough hiding places the males will kill one another. *Salaria pavo* has been bred in captivity many times. It prospers in sea or brackish water.

287

Shrimpfish [288] (*Aeoliscus strigatus*)

The Shrimpfish belongs to the family Centriscidae, which is distributed in the Pacific and Indian oceans. Their bodies are covered with bony armour. The tail is reduced and the dorsal fin protrudes backwards and forms a pointed end to the body. The fish of this family swim with their heads pointing down and their tails up. Most of them associate in small groups. In their natural habitat they live in association with sea-

288

urchins; the reason for this behaviour is still unknown. They acclimatize quickly in the aquarium and readily take dried or frozen brine shrimps which have been dipped in hot water to make them fall to the bottom. Small pieces of meat or crustaceans are also eaten.

289

Sprightly Dragonet [289] (*Callionymus festivus*)

This brightly coloured representative of the family Callionymidae occurs in the Mediterranean, Adriatic and Black seas. The male [289] grows to 14 cm in length. It lives at a depth of 1–3 metres and moves by darting suddenly over the sandy bottom. The spawning time is July to August. Females which are ready for spawning jerk their first dorsal fin. During the spawning act the pair swim to the surface where the fish eject their eggs and milt. Droplets of oil in nutritive yolk keep the eggs on the surface. In captivity the fish needs well-oxygenated water and feeds on various kinds of animal food. The fish like to catch tiny freshwater plankton, cyclops, water fleas, or benthonic animals, mainly small larval chironomid midges. The courtship of the female involves the male swimming round and round the female with its huge multi-coloured fins spread out.

Tripterygium nasus [290]

The fish belongs to the family Tripterygiidae. Distinctive features are three dorsal fins and a comparatively small pointed mouth. It inhabits the intertidal zone but it can be found also at a depth of 25 metres. Rocky places overgrown with thickets of various algae are its favourite environment. This species never seeks refuge, even if pursued, but just 'skips' on the rocks when disturbed.

290

The male [290] is about 7 cm long and displays a splendidly red colour in the spawning season. The head, throat and pelvic fins are black. The females are smaller and are inconspicuously light brown in colour. The eggs are laid on bare walls of rocks. The male protects a territory of about 4 metres in diameter around the brood. *Tripterygium nasus* is a common fish which occurs throughout the Mediterranean and Adriatic seas. In the aquarium it needs well-filtered and oxygenated water and its food should consist of small planktonic crustaceans, such as *Cyclops* and *Daphnia*. These should be given in small but frequent doses. It is very sensitive to any turbidity of the water and often dies for no apparent reason.

Shore Clingfish [291, 292] (*Lepadogaster lepadogaster*)

This is a member of the family of clingfishes (Gobiesocidae), which lack spines in the dorsal fin. On the ventral side of the body they have a sucking disc [292], which is formed by the pelvic and the pectoral fins and also by modified bones of the shoulder girdle. All species of this family are small fish which live in the intertidal zone of coastal waters and hide under stones. The sucking disc enables them to cling very firmly even to smooth rocks and to withstand the pounding of even the strongest

291

waves. The fish of the genus *Lepadogaster* can be found on the European coasts of the Black, Adriatic and Mediterranean seas and around the coasts of Great Britain. The Shore Clingfish grows to 7–12 cm in length. Adult specimens have a fringed skin fold

292

above the nasal openings. They are difficult to capture. It is often necessary to remove many stones from around the hiding place of the fish to get to the sandy bottom before working towards the centre to expose and catch it. It is advisable to put a stone on the net before inspecting it. The fish quickly moves on its sucking disc and tries to keep to the underside. This species is very resistant to the rigours of transportation. The Shore Clingfish is tolerant to other fish of the same species. They will live peacefully together among the stones scattered on the bed of the tank. They live on tubifex worms, larvae, or pupae of chironomid midges and pieces of fish and poultry meat. On one occasion five specimens were fed exclusively with lean pork for six months. They grew exceptionally well, even though this food is generally considered to be completely unsuitable for fish. Only with great difficulty did they later acclimatize to a varied diet. The species is easy to rear in captivity. The fish are hardy and aquarium specimens may live in excellent physical condition for many years.

BIBLIOGRAPHY

Allen, G. R.: *The Anemonenfishes* (Their Classification and Biology). T. F. H. Publ. Inc., Neptune, New Jersey, 1972.
Angel, F.: *Atlas des poissons*, Vol. IV: *Aquariophilie*. Paris, N. Boubée et Cie, 1970.
Arnold, P. – Ahl, E.: *Fremdländische Süsswasserfische*. Wenzel und Sohn, Brunswick, 1936.
Axelrod, H. R.: *Freshwaterfishes*, Book I. T. F. H. Publ. Inc., Neptune, New Jersey, USA, 1974.
Axelrod, H. R. – Burgess, W. E.: *African Cichlids of Lakes Malawi and Tanganyika*. 4th edition. T. F. H. Publ. Inc., Neptune, New Jersey, USA, 1976.
Axelrod, H. R., and others: *Exotic Tropical Fishes*. T. F. H. Publ. Inc., Neptune, Jersey City 2, New Jersey, USA, 1961.
Axelrod, H. R. – Emmens, C. W.: *Exotic Marine Fishes*. T. F. H. Publ. Inc., Jersey City 2, New Jersey, USA, 1969.
Axelrod, H. R. – Vorderwinkler, W.: *Salt-Water Aquarium Fishes*.T. F. H. Publ. Inc., Jersey City 2, New Jersey, USA, 1967.
Bade, E.: *Das Süsswasser-Aquarium*, 5th edition. F. Pfenningstorff, Berlin, 1934.
Baensch, H. A. –Riehl, R.: *Aquarien Atlas*, Vol. II. Mergus-Verlag, Melle, 1985.
Bath, H.: *Revision der Blenniini* (Pisces: Blenniidae). Senckerbergiana, Biologica, 57, 4/6, 167–234, 1977.
Beauchot, M. L. et R.: *La vie des poissons*. Paris, Stock, 1976.
Bech, R.: *Eierlegende Zahnkarpfen*. Neumann Verlag, Leipzig – Radebeul, 1984.
Breder, Ch. M. – Rosen, D. E.: *Modes of Reproduction in Fishes*. T. F. H. Publ. Inc., Neptune, New Jersey, USA, 1966.
Brichard, P.: *Das grosse Buch der Tanganjika Cichliden*. Bede Verlag D-8371 Kollnburg, Copyright T. F. H. Publ. Inc., 1992.
Cust, G.: *Guide des poissons et de l'aguarium tropical*. Lausanne, Édition de la Tête de Feuilles, 1976.
Dahlstrom, P.- Schiotz, A.: *Aquarium Fishes*. Collins, 1972.
Emmens, C. W.: *How to Keep and Breed Tropical Fish*. T. F. H. Publ. Inc., 1962.
Frank, S.: *The Pictoral Encyclopedia of Fish*. Hamlyn, 1969.
Franke, H.-J.: *Handbuch der Wels-Kunde*. Urania Verlag, Leipzig – Jena – Berlin, 1985.
Fourmanoir, P. – Laboute, P.: *Poissons des mers tropicales*. Papeete et Paris, Éditions du Pacifique et Hachette, 1976.
Fryer, G. – Iles, T. D.: *The Cichlid Fishes of the Great Lakes of Africa*. T. F. H. Publ. Inc., Neptune, New Jersey, 1972.
Géry, J.: *Characoids of the World*. T. F. H. Publ. Inc., Neptune, New Jersey, USA, 1978.
Goldstein, R. J.: *Cichlids*. T. F. H. Publ. Inc., Neptune, New Jersey, USA, 1971.
Hervey, G. H. – Hems, J.: *A Guide to Freshwater Aquarium Fishes*. Hamlyn, London, 1973.
Holly, M. – Meinken, H. – Rachow, A.: *Die Aquarienfische in Wort und Bild*. Alfred-Kernen-Verlag, Stuttgart, 1932–67
Hvass, H.: *Les poissons du monde entier*. Paris, F. Nathan, 1970.
Innes, W. T.: *Exotic Aguarium Fishes*. 17th edition. Innes Publishing Company, Philadelphia, 1954.
Jacobs, K.: *Die lebendgebärenden Fische der Süssgewässer*. VEB Edition, Leipzig, 1969.
Klausewitz, W. – Peyronel, B. – Tortonese, E. – Vesco, V. D.: *Life in the Aquarium*. Octopus, London, 1974.
Luther, W. – Fiedler, K.: *Die Unterwasserfauna der Mittelmeerküste*. 2nd edition. Verlag Paul Parey, Hamburg – Berlin, 1967.
Mclnerny, D. – Gerard, G.: *All About Tropical Fish*. Harrap, 1966.
Madsen, J. M.: *Aquarium Fishes in Colour*. Blandford, 1974.
Mayland, H. J.: *Complete Home Aquarium*. Ward Lock, 1976.
Mayland, H. J.: *Grosse Aquarienpraxis*. Vol. I: *Aquarium-Pflanzen-Fische*. Landbuch-Verlag, Hanover, 1977.
Mayland, H. J.: *Grosse Aquarienpraxis*. Vol. II: *Tropische Aquarienfische*. Landbuch-Verlag, Hanover, 1979.
Mayland, H. J.: *Grosse Aquarienpraxis*. Vol. III: *Cichliden und Fischzucht*. Landbuch-Verlag, Hanover, 1978.
Pinter, H.: *Handbuch der Aquarienfisch-Zucht*. Alfred-Kernen-Verlag, Stuttgart, 1966.
Richter, H. – J.: *Das Buch der Labyrinthfische*. Neumann Verlag, Leipzig – Radebeul, 1979.
Riehl, R.: *Fauna und Flora der Adria*. Verlag Paul Parey, Hamburg – Berlin, 1970.
Riehl, R. – Baensch, H. A.: *Aquarien Atlas*. Vol. I. Mergus-Verlag, Melle, 1983.
Riehl, R. – Baensch, H. A.: *Aquarien Atlas*. Vol. III. Mergus-Verlag, Melle, 1990.
Sagar, K.: *World Encyclopedia of Tropical Fish*. Octopus, London, 1978.
Scheel, J.: *Rivulins of the Old World*. T. F. H. Publ., Inc., Jersey City 2, New Jersey, 1968.
Simister, W.: *Home Aquarium Book*. David and Charles, 1976.
Sterba, G.: *Süsswasserfische aus aller Welt*. 3rd edition. Urania-Verlag, Leipzig – Jena – Berlin, 1977.
Sterba, G.: *Süsswasserfische der Welt*. Urania-Verlag, Leipzig – Jena – Berlin, 1987.
Vierke, J.: *Labyrinthfische und verwandte Arten*. Engelbert Pfriem Verlag, Wuppertal – Elberfeld, 1978.
Walker, B: *Marine Tropical Fish in Colour*. Blandford, 1975.
Walls, J. G.: *Fishes of the Northern Gulf of Mexico*. T. F. H. Publ. Inc., Neptune, 1975.
Wheeler, A.: *Fishes of the World*. Macmillan Publ. Co., Inc., New York, 1975.

INDEX OF COMMON NAMES

(Bold figures refer to main entries, figures in italics to numbers of illustrations.)

Algae-eater, Chinese **78-79**, 78-79/*87*, *88*
Amblydoras, Hancock's **83**, 82-83/*91*, *92*
Anemone Fish, Clown **222**, 222/*258*
Anemone Fish, Yellow-tailed **224**, 224/*261*
Angelfish, Black **236**, 237/*278*
Angelfish, Blue King **231**, 231/*270*
Angelfish, Emperor **230-231**, 230/*268*, *269*
Angelfish, Half-moon **233**, 233/*273*
Angelfish, Ringed Emperor **231**, 231/*270*
Angelfish, Speckled **236**, 236/*277*
Aphyosemion, Cape Lopez Lyretail **91-92**, 92/*102*, 95
Aphyosemion, Christy's **96**, 96/*107*
Aphyosemion, Plumed **97**, 97/*109*
Aphyosemion, Red **99**, 99/*113*
Aphyosemion, Red-chinned **96**, 96/*108*
Aphyosemion, Red-spotted **92-93**, 92/*103*
Aphyosemion, Scheel's **100**, 100/*114*
Aphyosemion, Steel-blue 90/100, 91, **93-95**, 93-95/*104*, *105*, *106*
Aphyosemion, Walker's **98**, 98-99/*110*, *111*, *112*
Aplocheilus, Striped **114-115**, 115/*132*, *133*
Argus-fish **221**, 221/*257*
Argus, Red 221
Arowana **194**, 194/225

Badis **154**, 154/*176*
Barb, Black-spot **68-69**, 68/*76*
Barb, Ember **58-59**, 58/*64*
Barb, Fireglow **58-59**, 58/*64*
Barb, Five-banded **59**, 59/*65*
Barb, Golden **64**, 64/*71*
Barb, Nigger 69/*78*, **70**
Barb, Odessa 68/*77*, **69**
Barb, Purple-headed 69/*78*, **70**
Barb, Rosy 48/52
Barb, Schubert's 64, 64/*71*
Barb, Spanner **60**, 61/*67*
Barb, Stoliczka's **64**, 65/*72*
Barb, Striped **66-67**, 66-67/*73*, *74*, *75*
Barb, Sumatra **62**, 62-63/*68*, *69*, *70*
Barb, Tiger **62**, 62-63/*68*, *70*
Barb, Twospot 69
Barb, Zebra **66-67**, 66-67/*73*, *74*, *75*
Barb, Black Ruby 69/*78*, **70**
Bass, Painted Coral 202-203/*233*, *234*, **203-204**
Beacon-fish **21**, 21/*19*
Black-tailed Humbug 225
Blenny, Adrian 240
Blenny, Bloodthirsty **241**, 241/*284*
Blenny, Cat's **242**, 242/*285*
Blenny, Dalmatian 240
Blenny, Dark-striped **240**, 240/*283*
Blenny, Eyed **243**, 243/*286*
Blenny, Sphinx **242**, 243/*287*
Blenny, Tentacle **238-239**, 239/*282*
Blenny, Tompot 241
Blenny, Zvonimir's 241

Bloodfin **33**, 33/*33*
Blowfish, White-spotted **234**, 235/*276*
Bluehead **208**, 208/*239*, *240*
Blue Streak 209
Botia, Tiger **80**, 80/*89*
Brown Gaper **204**, 204/*235*
Bullhead, Common **88**, 88/*97*
Bullhead, Marbled **88**, 88/*97*
Butterfly-fish **194-195**, 195/*226*
Butterfly Fish, Banded **214**, 215/*249*
Butterfly Fish, Common **218**, 219/*254*
Butterfly Fish, Emperor **218**, 219/*255*
Butterfly Fish, Flag **217**, 217/*252*
Butterfly Fish, Four-eyed **218**, 218/*253*
Butterfly Fish, Half-masked **217**, 216/*251*
Butterfly Fish, Long-nosed **217**, 216/*250*
Butterfly Fish, Threadfin **217**, 217/252

Catfish, Armoured 85
Cave-fish, Blind **32**, 32/*31*
Characin, Arnold's Red-eyed **11**, 11/*6*
Characin, Fanning **38-39**, 38/*40*
Characin, Long-finned **9-10**, 9-10/*3*, *4*, 11
Characin, Swordtailed **34-35**, 35/*36*
Chromide, Green 163
Chromide, Orange **163**, 163/*188*
Cichlid, Barred **142-143**, 143/*165*
Cichlid, Borelli's Dwarf **148**, 148/*170*
Cichlid, Convict **139-141**, 139-141/*161*, *162*, *163*
Cichlid, Five-spot African **160**, 160/*184*
Cichlid, Flag **142-143**, 143/*165*, 146/*168*, **147**
Cichlid, Oscar's **154-155**, 155/*177*
Cichlid, Ramirez's Dwarf **152**, 152-153/*174*, *175*
Cichlid, Red 147, 147/169
Cichlid, Red Dwarf **160-161**, 161-162/*185*, *186*, *187*
Cichlid, Ring-tailed Pike **170-171**, 170/*196*
Cichlid, Thomas's Dwarf **165-167**, 165-166/*190*, *191*, *192*
Cichlid, Velvet **154-155**, 155/*177*
Cichlid, Yellow Dwarf **149**, 149/*171*
Cichlid, Zebra 138, **139-141**, 139-141/*161*, *162*, *163*
Cleanerfish, Four-blue-streak **209**, 209/*241*
Clingfish, Shore **247-248**, 247-248/*291*, *292*
Clown, Gold-finned **222-223**, 223/*260*
Clown, Red **222**, 223/*259*
Clown, Saddle Back 222
Cod, Fairy 202-203/*233*, *234*, **203-204**
Corydoras, Dwarf 86/*95*, **87**
Corydoras, Rabaut's 86/*95*, **87**
Corydoras, Schultze's **87**, 87/*96*

Damselfish, Marginate **227**, 227/*264*
Damselfish, Three-spot **226-227**, 226/*263*

Damselfish, White-tailed **225**, 225/*262*
Danio, Blue **52**, 52/*56*
Danio, Giant **55-56**, 55-57/*61*, *62*, *63*
Danio, Leopard 53, 53/*58*
Danio, Pearl **51**, 51/*55*, 53
Danio, Spotted **54**, 54/*60*
Danio, Zebra **52-53**, 52-53/*57*, *59*, 54, 55
Demon Fish **151**, 151/*173*
Devil, Blue **228**, 228/*266*
Devil, Neon **228**, 228/*265*
Discus, Blue **145**, 145/*167*
Discus, Cobalt Blue 145
Discus, Brown **144**, 144/*166*, 145
Discus, Green 145
Discus, Red 145
Discus, Royal Blue 145
Discus, Yellow-brown **144**, 144/*166*
Dragonet, Sprightly **245**, 245/*289*

Eartheater **151**, 151/*173*
Epiplatys, Banded **108-109**, 109/*124*
Epiplatys, Fire-mouth **106-107**, 107-108/*122*, *123*
Epiplatys, Six-barred **109**, 109/*125*

Fairy Cod 202-203/*233*, *234*, **203-204**
Fairy Basslet **213**, 213/*245*
Festivum **142-143**, 143/*165*
Fighting Fish, Pacific **183-184**, 183/*211*
Fighting Fish, Siamese **181-182**, 181-182/*208*, *209*, *210*
Filefish, Red-toothed 232/*272*, **233**
Firefish, Fight **236-237**, 237/*279*
Firefish, Red 236
Flying Fox **73**, 73/*82*
Flying Fox, Siamese **74**, 74/*83*

Goby, Bucchichi's **238**, 239/*281*
Goby, Knight **201**, 201/*232*
Goby, Snakehead **238**, 238/*280*
Goby, Striped **238**, 239/*281*
Goldfish **49**, 49/*53*
'Goldneon' 39
Gourami, Banded **184**, 185/*213*
Gourami, Blue 175, 177/*203*
Gourami, Dwarf 174/*200*, 175
Gourami, Dwarf Croaking **189-190**, 190/*220*
Gourami, Giant **184**, 185/*213*
Gourami, Moonlight 177
Gourami, Mosaic **179-180**, 178-180/*204*, *205*, *206*, *207*
Gourami, Pearl **179-180**, 178-180/*204*, *205*, *206*, *207*
Gourami, Schaller's 190, 190/*221*
Gourami, Snake-skinned 177
Gourami, Striped **184**, 185/*213*
Gourami, Thick-lipped **184**, 184/*212*
Gourami, Three-spot **175-177**, 175-177/*201*, *202*, *203*
Gramma, Royal **213**, 213/*245*
Grouper, Lyretail **203-204**, 202-203/*233*, *234*
Gularis, Blue **100-101**, 101/*115*
Guppy **133**, 132-133/*154*, *155*

Harlequin Fish 70/*79*, **71**
Hatchetfish, Common 47, 47/*51*
Hatchetfish, Marbled 46, 46/*50*, 47

Head-and-tail-light Fish **21**, 21/*19*

Jewelfish **147**, 147/*169*

Killifish, Venezuela **123**, 123/*143*
Knife-fish, African **196**, 196/*227*
Kribensis **160-161**, 161-162/*185*, *186*, *187*

Ladiges' Gaucho **120**, 120/*138*
Loach, Clown **80**, 80/*89*
Loach, Cross-banded **80-81**, 81/*90*
Longfin, Peruvian **123**, 122/*142*
Lyretail, Calabar **105**, 105/*120*
Lyretail, Cape Lopez **91-92**, 92/*102*
Lyretail, Plumed **97**, 97/*109*
Lyretail, Red **99**, 99/*113*

Minnow, Pike Top **135**, 135/*157*
Minnow, White Cloud Mountain **72**, 72/*81*
Mollienesia, 'Black' 135
Mollienesia, 'Lyre' 135
Mollienesia, 'Veil' 135
Molly, Sail-fin **134-135**, 134/*156*
Mouthbreeder, Southern **167**, 167/*193*

Needles, Freshwater 192/*203*, 193
Nothobranch, Beira **112**, 112/*128*
Nothobranch, Green **113-114**, 113-114/*130*, *131*
Nothobranch, Guenther's 110-111/*126*, *127*, **111**
Nothobranch, Rachow's **112**, 113/*129*

Painted Coral Bass **203-204**, 203/*233*, *234*
Panchax, Blue **116**, 116/*134*
Panchax, Lamp-eyed **116-117**, 117/*135*
Panchax, Playfair's **102**, 102-103/*116*, *117*, *118*
Panchax, Red-chinned **106-107**, 107-108/*122*, *123*
Panchax, Sheljuzhko's **106**, 106/*121*
Panchax, Striped **108-109**, 109/*124*
Paradise-fish **186-187**, 186-187/*215*, *216*, *217*, 188
Paradise-fish, Black **188**, 188-189/*218*, *219*
Pearl Fish, Black-finned **121-122**, 121-122/*140*, *141*
Pencilfish, Ansorge's African **43**, 43/*46*
Pencilfish, Barred **42-43**, 42/*45*
Pencilfish, Dwarf **40**, 40/*42*, 41
Pencilfish, Espe's **42-43**, 42/*45*
Pencilfish, Tail-eye **44**, 44/*47*
Pencilfish, Three-banded **41-42**, 41-42/*43*, *44*
Pencilfish, Tube-mouthed **44-45**, 45/*48*, *49*
Penguin Fish **36**, 37/*38*
Perch, Marbled Climbing **191**, 191/*222*
Perch, Sharp-nosed **191**, 191/*222*
Platy, 'Calico' **130-131**, 131/*153*
Platy, 'Comet' **129**, 129/*151*
Platy, 'Meri-gold' **128**, 128/*149*
Platy, 'Parrot' 128
Platy, 'Red' **124**, 124/*144*, **128-129**, 129/*150*
Platy, 'Tuxedo' **130**, 130/*152*
Platy, 'Wagtail' 131
Platy, wild 128
Poor Man's Moorish Idol **220**, 220/*256*
Port Hoplo **84-85**, 84-85/*93*, *94*

Puffer, Black-spotted **234**, 235/*275*
Puffer, Sharp-nosed **234**, 234/*274*
Pyrrhulina, Rachow's **38-39**, 38/*40*

Rainbowfish, Black-lined **198-199**, 199/*230*
Rainbowfish, Boeseman's **193**, 193/*224*
Rainbowfish, Dwarf **198-199**, 199/*230*
Rasbora, Pearly **71**, 71/*80*
Rasbora, Red 70/*79*, **71**
'Red Oscar' 155
Reef Fish, Orange-tailed **229**, 229/*267*
Rivulus, Colombia **118-119**, 118-119/*136*, *137*
Roloffia, Gery's **104**, 104/*119*

Scalar, Amazonian 136, 136/*158*, 150/*172*, **151**
Scat-fish **221**, 221/*257*
'Shark', Bala **75**, 75/84
'Shark', Black 77
'Shark', Bridle **77**, 77/*86*
'Shark', Red-tailed Black **76**, 76/*85*
Shrimpfish **244-245**, 244/*288*
Spiny Eel **197**, 197/*228*
Squirrelfish, Sabre **214**, 215/*248*
Stickleback, Three-spined **200**, 200/*231*
Sunfish, Pumpkinseed **156**, 156/*178*
Surgeonfish, White-throated **232**, 232/*271*
Swordtail, 'Lyre' **126-127**, 127/*147*
Swordtail, 'Tuxedo' **126**, 126/*146*
Swordtail, 'Wagtail' **125**, 125/*145*
Swordtail, wild 127

Tetra, Black-line 12, 12/*7*
Tetra, Black Phantom 34
Tetra, Bleeding Heart 20/*17*, *18*, **21**
Tetra, Bleher's **26**, 26/*25*
Tetra, Bucktoothed **32-33**, 33/*32*
Tetra, Buenos Aires **23**, 23/*21*
Tetra, Cardinal **31**, 31/*30*
Tetra, Congo **10-11**, 11/*5*
Tetra, Diamond **34**, 35/*35*
Tetra, Flag **19**, 19/*16*
Tetra, Flame**17-18**, 17-18/*13*, *14*, 19
Tetra, from Rio **17-18**, 17-18/*13*, *14*, 19
Tetra, Garnet **22**, 22/*20*
Tetra, Glow-light **23-24**, 23-24/*22*, *23*
Tetra, Griem's **19**, **19**/*15*
Tetra, Jewel 13,14/*9*
Tetra, Lemon **15**, 15/*11*
Tetra, Neon 8/*2*, **28-29**, 28-30/*27*, *28*, *29*
Tetra, Perez 20/*17*, *18*, **21**
Tetra, Peruvian16, 16/*12*
Tetra, Pink Jewelled**14-15**, 14/*10*
Tetra, Pretty **22**, 22/*20*
Tetra, Red **17-18**, 17-18/*13*, *14*
Tetra, Red-headed **26**, 27/*26*
Tetra, Red-nosed 26
Tetra, Red Phantom **34**, 34/*34*
Tetra, Rummy-nosed 26
Tetra, Scholze's **12**, 12/*7*
Tetra, Serpae **13**, 13/*8*
Tetra, Silver-tipped **25**, 25/*24*
Tetra, Weitzman's **36**, 36/*37*
Tilapia, Maria's 156/*179*, **157**
Toby, Ocellated **234**, 234/*274*

Veiltail **50**, 50/*54*

Wrasse, Ashy 206
Wrasse, Black-tail 207
Wrasse, Blue-grey **211**, 211/*243*
Wrasse, Doederlein's **207**, 208/*238*
Wrasse, Five-spot **206**, 206/*237*
Wrasse, Green-eyed **205**, 205/*236*
Wrasse, Mediterranean 205
Wrasse, Mediterranean Bluehead **214**, 214/*247*
Wrasse, Rainbow **212**, 212/*244*
Wrasse, Yellowhead **213**, 213/*246*

INDEX OF SCIENTIFIC NAMES

(Bold figures refer to main entries, figures in italics to numbers of illustrations.)

Abudefduf oxyodon **228**, 228/*265*
Acanthurus leucosternon **232**, 232/*271*
Aeoliscus strigatus **244-245**, 244/*288*
Aequidens curviceps **147**, 146/*168*
Aidablennius sphynx **242**, 243/*287*
Amblydoras hancocki **83**, 82-83/*91*, *92*
Ameiurus nebulosus **88**, 88/*97*
Amphiprion frenatus **222**, 223/*259*, 223
Amphiprion latifasciatus **224**, 224/*261*
Amphiprion ocellaris **222**, 222/*258*
Amphiprion polymnus 222
Amphiprion sebae **222-223**, 223/*260*
Amphiprion xanthurus 224
Anomalochromis thomasi **165-167**, 165-166/*190*, *191*, *192*
Anoptichthys jordani **31**, 31/*30*
Aphyocharax anisitsi 33, 33/*33*
Aphyosemion ahli 96
Aphyosemion australe **91-92**, 92/*102*, 95
Aphyosemion australe hjerreseni **91-92**, 91/*101*
Aphyosemion bivittatum **99**, 99/*133*
Aphyosemion bivittatum holyi 99
Aphyosemion 'burundi' 100
Aphyosemion calliurum **96**, 96/*108*
Aphyosemion calliurum ahli 93
Aphyosemion calliurum calliurum 93
Aphyosemion christyi **96**, 96/*107*
Aphyosemion coeruleum 100
Aphyosemion filamentosum **97**, 97/*109*
Aphyosemion gardneri 90/*100*, 91, **93-95**, 92-95/*104*, *105*, *106*
Aphyosemion gulare coeruleum 100
Aphyosemion loennbergi 99
Aphyosemion lujae **92-93**, 92/*103*
Aphyosemion multicolor 99
Aphyosemion nigerianum 93
Aphyosemion pappenheimi 99
Aphyosemion riggenbachi 99
Aphyosemion scheeli **100**, 100/*114*
Aphyosemion sjoestedti **100-101**, 101/*115*
Aphyosemion splendopleure 99
Aphyosemion unistrigatum 99
Aphyosemion vexillifer 96
Aphyosemion walkeri **98**, 98-99/*110*, *111*, *112*
Apistogramma borellii **148**, 148/*170*
Apistogramma reitzigi **149**, 149/*171*
Aplocheilichthus macrophthalmus 116, 117
Aplocheilus lineatus **114-115**, 115/*132*, *133*
Aplocheilus lucescens 116
Aplocheilus mattei 116
Aplocheilus panchax panchax 116, 116/*134*
Aplocheilus panchax siamensis 116
Aplocheilus rubropunctatus 116
Arapaima gigas 194
Arnoldichthys spilopterus **11**, 11/*6*
Arothron hispidus **234**, 235/*276*
Arothron nigropunctatus **234**, 234/*275*
Arusetta asfur **233**, 233/*273*, 236

Astatotilapia burtoni **164**, 164/*180*
Astronotus ocellatus **154-155**, 155/*177*
Astyanax fasciatus mexicanus 32
Austrofundulus dolichopterus 123
Austrofundulus myersi 123
Austrofundulus transilis **123**, 123/*143*

Badis badis **154**, 154/*176*
Balantiocheilus melanopterus **75**, 75/*84*
Barbus barilioides 60, 60/*66*
Barbus conchonius 48, 48/52
Barbus fasciatus **58-59**, 58/*64*
Barbus filamentosus **68-69**, 68/*76*
Barbus lateristriga **60**, 61/*67*
Barbus lineatus **66-67**, 66-67/*73*, *74*, *75*
Barbus mahecola 69
Barbus nigrofasciatus 69/*78*, **70**
Barbus pentazona pentazona **59**, 59/*65*
Barbus 'schuberti' **64**, 64/*71*
Barbus semifasciolatus 64
Barbus sp. 68/*77*, **69**
Barbus stoliczkanus **64**, 65/*72*
Barbus ticto 69
Barbus tetrazona **62**, 62-63/*68*, *69*, *70*
Bedotia geayi **198**, 198/*229*
Belonesox belizanus **135**, 135/*157*
Betta imbellis **183-184**, 183/*211*
Betta splendens **181-182**, 181-182/*208-210*
Botia macracantha **80**, 80/*89*
Botia striata **80-81**, 81/*90*
Brachydanio albolineatus **51**, 51/*55*, 52
Branchydanio frankei 53, 53/*58*
Brachydanio kerri **52**, 52/*56*
Brachydanio nigrofasciatus **54**, 54/*60*
Brachydanio rerio **52-53**, 52-53/*57*, *59*
Brycinus longipinnis **9-10**, 9-10/*3*, *4*

Calichthys calichthys 85
Callionymus festivus **245**, 245/*289*
Canthigaster solandri **234**, 234/*274*
Carassius auratus auratus **49**, 49/*53*
Carassius auratus var. *bicaudatus* **50**, 50/*54*
Carnegiella strigata **46**, 46/*50*
Chaetodon auriga **217**, 217/252
Chaetodon capistratus **218**, 218/*253*
Chaetodon semilarvatus 216/*251*, **217**
Chaetodon striatus **214**, 215/*249*
Chaetodontoplus mesoleucus **218**, 219/*255*
Cheirodon axelrodi **31**, 31/*30*
Cheirodon leuciscus 31
Cheirodon meinkeni 31
Cheirodon piaba 31
Chelmon rostratus 216/*250*, **217**
Chromidotilapia guentheri 157
Chromidotilapia kingsleyae **157**, 157/*180*
Cichlasoma festivum **142-143**, 143/*165*
Cichlasoma nigrofasciatum **139-141**, 139-141/*161*, *162*, *163*

Cichlasoma nigrofasciatum x *C. spilurum* **142**, 142/*164*
Cichlasoma spilurum 137-138/*159*, *160*, **138**, 139
Colisa chuna **185-186**, 185/*214*
Colisa fasciata **184**, 185/*213*
Colisa labiosa **184**, 184/*212*
Colisa lalia 174/*200*, 175
Coris formosa **211**, 211/*243*
Coris gaimard 211
Coris giofredi 212
Coris julis **212**, 212/*244*
Corydoras myersi 87
Corydoras rabauti 86/*95*, 87
Corydoras schultzei **87**, 87/*96*
Corydoras zygatus 87
Crenicichla saxatilis **170-171**, 170/*196*
Crenilabrus cinereus 206
Crenilabrus doederleini **207**, 208/*238*
Crenilabrus mediterraneus 205
Crenilabrus ocellatus **205**, 205/*236*
Crenilabrus quinquemaculatus **206**, 205/*237*
Ctenopoma oxyrhynchus **191**, 191/*222*
Cynolebias nigripinnis **121-122**, 121-122/*140*, *141*
Cynolebias whitei **120**, 121/*139*
Cynopoecilus ladigesi **120**, 120/*138*

Danio aequipinnatus **55-56**, 55-57/*61*, *62*, *63*
Dascyllus albisella 226
Dascyllus aruanus **225**, 225/*262*
Dascyllus marginatus **227**, 227/*264*
Dascyllus melanurus 225
Dascyllus trimaculatus **226-227**, 226/*263*

Epalzeorhynchus kallopterus **73**, 73/*82*
Epalzeorhynchus siamensis **74**, 74/*83*
Epiplatys chaperi 106, 107
Epiplatys chaperi sheljuzhkoi **106**, 106/*121*
Epiplatys dageti dageti 107
Epiplatys dageti monroviae **106-107**, 107-108/*122*, *123*
Epiplatys fasciolatus **108-109**, 109/*124*
Epiplatys sexfasciatus **109**, 109/*125*
Etroplus maculatus **163**, 163/*188*
Etroplus suratensis 163
Exodon paradoxus **32-33**, 33/*32*

Gasteropelecus sternicla **47**, 47/*51*
Gasterosteus aculeatus **200**, 200/*231*
Geophagus jurupari **151**, 151/*173*
Glossolepis incisus 2/*1*
Glyphidodontops cyaneus **228**, 228/*266*, **229**
Glyphidodontops hemicyaneus **229**, 229/*267*
Gobius bucchichii **238**, 239/*281*
Gobius ophiocephalus **238**, 238/*280*
Gramma hemichrysos **213**, 213/*245*
Gyrinocheilus kaznakovi **78-79**, 78-79/*87*, *88*

Halichoeres garnoti **213**, 213/*246*
Halichoeres maculipinna **213**
Haplochromis desfontainesi 164
Hasemania nana **25**, 25/*24*
Hemichromis bimaculatus 147, 147/*169*
Hemigrammus bleheri **26**, 26/*25*
Hemigrammus caudovittatus **23**, 23/*21*
Hemigrammus erythrozonus **23-24**, 23-24/*22*, *23*
Hemigrammus ocellifer, falsus, 21
Hemigrammus ocellifer ocellifer **21**, 21/*19*
Hemigrammus pulcher **22**, 22/*20*
Hemigrammus rhodostomus 26
Heniochus acuminatus **220**, 220/*256*
Herotilapia multispinosa 158-159/*181*, *182*, *183*, **159**
Hoplosternum thoracatum **84-85**, 84-85/*93*, *94*
Hyphessobrycon callistus **13**, 14/*9*
Hyphessobrycon erythrostigma 20/*17*, *18*, **21**
Hyphessobrycon flammeus **17-18**, 17-18/*13*, *14*
Hyphessobrycon griemi **19**, 19/*15*
Hyphessobrycon heterorhabdus **19**, 19/*16*
Hyphessobrycon ornatus 13, **14-15**, 14/*10*, 21
Hyphessobrycon peruvianus **16**, 16/*12*
Hyphessobrycon pulchripinnis **15**, 15/*11*
Hyphessobrycon rubrostigma 21
Hyphessobrycon scholzei **12**, 12/*7*
Hyphessobrycon serpae **13**, 13/*8*

Labaricus quadrilineatus **209**, 209/*241*, 210
Labeo bicolor **76**, 76/*85*, 77
Labeo frenatus **77**, 77/*86*
Labidochromis coeruleus **172**, 172/*198*
Labroides dimidiatus 209, 210/*242*, 231
Lepadogaster lepadogaster **247-248**, 247- 248/*291*, *292*
Lepomis gibbosus **156**, 156/*178*
Limnochromis auritus **173**, 173/*199*
Lipophrys adriaticus 240
Lipophrys canevae **242**, 242/*285*
Lipophrys dalmatinus 240

Macrognathus aculeatus **197**, 197/*228*
Macropodus opercularis concolor **188**, 188-189/*218*, *219*
Macropodus opercularis opercularis **186-187**, 186-187/*215*, *216*, *217*
Megalamphodus megalopterus 34
Megalamphodus sweglesi **34**, 34/*34*
Melanochromis brevis **171**, 171/*197*, 172
Melanotaenia boesemani **193**, 193/*224*
Melanotaenia maccullochi **198-199**, 199/*230*
Moenkhausia pittieri **34**, 35/*35*
Morulius chrysophekadion 77

Nannocharax ansorgei **43**, 43/*46*
Nannostomus espei **42-43**, 42/*45*
Nannostomus marginatus **40**, 40/*42*
Nannostomus trifasciatus **41-42**, 41-42/*43*, *44*
Neolebias trilineatus **39**, 39/*41*
Nothobranchius guentheri 110-111/*126*, *127*, **111**, 112
Nothobranchius korthausae **113-114**, 113-114/*130*, *131*
Nothobranchius melanospilus **112**, 112/*128*
Nothobranchius taeniopygus **112**, 113/*129*

Odonus niger 232/*272*, **233**
Osteoglossum bicirrhosum **194**, 194/225

Pachypanchax playfairi **102**, 102-103/*116*, *117*, *118*

Pangasius sanitwongsei 89
Pangasius sutchi **89**, 89/*99*
Pantodon buchholzi **194-195**, 195/*226*
Papiliochromis ramirezi **152**, 152-153/*174, 175,* **165**
Parablennius gattorugine 241
Parablennius rouxi **240**, 240/*283*
Parablennius tentacularis **238-239**, 239/*282*
Parachaetodon ocellatus **218**, 219/*254*
Paracheirodon innesi 8/2, **28-29**, 28-30/*27, 28, 29*
Paratilapia auritus 173
Pelmatochromis annectens 160
Pelmatochromis arnoldi 160
Pelmatochromis auritus 173
Pelvicachromis aureocephalus 161
Pelvicachromis kribensis 161
Pelvicachromis pulcher **160-161**, 161-162/*185, 186, 187*
Pelvicachromis subocellatus 161
Pelvicachromis taeniatus 161
Petitella georgiae 26, 27/*26*
Phenacogrammus interruptus **10-11**, 11/*5*
Pictiblennius sanguinolentus **241**, 241/*284*
Pictiblennius zvonimiri 241
Pimelodus ornatus **88**, 88/*98*
Poecilia latipinna 135
Poecilia reticulata 132-133/*154, 155,* **133**
Poecilia sphenops 135
Poecilia velifera **134-135**, 134/*156*
Poecilobrycon eques 42, **44-45**, 45/*48, 49*
Poecilobrycon unifasciatus ocellatus **44**, 44/*47*
Poecilocharax weitzmani **36**, 36/*37*
Pomacanthodes annularis **231**, 231/*270*
Pomacanthodes imperator **230-231**, 230/*268, 269*
Pomacanthodes maculosus **236**, 236/*277*
Pomacanthus arcuatus **236**, 237/*278*
Pomacanthus paru 236
Procatopus similis **116-117**, 117/*135*
Pseudocrenilabrus philander dispersus **167**, 167/*193*
Pseudotropheus auratus 168/*194,* **169**
Pseudotropheus zebra **169**, 169/*195*
Pterois miles **236-237**, 237/*279*
Pterois volitans 236
Pterolebias peruensis 122/*142,* **123**
Pterophyllum scalare *136,* 136/*158,* 150/*172,* **151**
Pyrrhulina rachoviana **38-39**, 38/*40*

Rasbora heteromorpha 70/*79,* **71**
Rasbora vateriflorís **71**, 71/*80*
Rivulus elegans 118
Rivulus milesi **118-119**, 118-119/*136, 137*
Rivulus urophthalmus 118
Roloffia geryi **104**, 104/*119*
Roloffia liberiensis **105**, 105/*120*
Roloffia roloffi 104

Salaria pavo **243**, 243/*286*
Sargocentron spiniferum **214**, 215/*248*
Scatophagus argus **221**, 221/*257*
Scatophagus argus rubrifrons 221
Scatophagus tetracanthus 221
Selenotoca multifasciata 221
Serranelus hepatus **204**, 204/*235*
Stevardia riisei **34-35**, 35/*36*
Stigmatogobius sadanundio **201**, 201/*232*
Symphodus melanocerus 207
Symphysodon aequifasciatus 145
Symphysodon aequifasciatus axelrodi **144**, 144/*166,* 145
Symphysodon aequifasciatus haraldi **145**, 145/*167*
Symphysodon discus 145
Syngnathus pulchellus 192/*203,* 193

Tanichthys albonubes **72**, 72/*81*
Thalassoma bifasciatum **208**, 208/*239, 240*
Thalassoma pavo 214, 214/*247*
Thayeria boehlkei **36-37**, 37/*39*
Thayeria obliqua **36**, 37/*38*
Thayeria sanctaemariae 36
Thysia ansorgei **160**, 160/*184*
Tilapia mariae 156/*179,* 157
Trichogaster leeri 178-180/*204, 205 206, 207,* **179-180**
Trichogaster microlepis 177
Trichogaster pectoralis 177
Trichogaster trichopterus **175-177**, 175-177/*201, 203, 204*
Trichogaster trichopterus 'Cosby' 176
Trichogaster trichopterus sumatranus 175, 177/*203*
Trichopsis pumilus **189-190**, 190/*220*
Trichopsis schalleri **190**, 190/*221*
Trichopsis vittatus 189
Tripterygium nasus **246**, 246/*290*

Variola louti 202-203/*233, 234,* **203-204**

Xenomystus nigri **196**, 196/*227*
Xiphophorus helleri **125**, 125/*145,* **126**, 126-127/*146, 147, 148*
Xiphophorus maculatus **128-129**, 129/*151*
Xiphophorus maculatus var. *sanquinea* 124/*144,* 125, **128-129**, 129/*150*
Xiphophorus variatus **128**, 128/*149*

Picture Acknowledgements

Biegner, Bedřich: 94
Chlupaty, Peter: 243, 250, 271
Chvojka, Milan: 18, 22, 32, 50, 51, 67, 78, 82, 87, 88, 93, 113, 121, 125, 153, 188, 225, 239, 240, 241, 242, 245, 258, 259, 260, 262, 263, 264, 265, 266, 267, 268, 272, 273, 274, 279
Čihař, Jiří: 254, 255, 261, 270, 275, 278, 288
Contardo, Pavel: 71, 76, 86, 89, 176, 257
Eliáš, Jaroslav: 2, 7, 13, 15, 23, 24, 27, 28, 42, 52, 57, 58, 62, 63, 73, 74, 75, 83, 84, 91, 92, 98, 100, 105, 106, 110, 111, 143, 144, 152, 158, 162, 163, 168, 172, 173, 216, 217
Frank, Stanislav: 1a, 3, 4, 5, 6, 8, 9, 10, 11, 12, 16, 17, 19, 20, 21, 25, 26, 31, 33, 34, 35, 36, 37, 38, 39, 40, 43, 44, 45, 46, 47, 48, 49, 56, 59, 60, 61, 64, 65, 66, 68, 69, 77, 79, 80, 81, 95, 96, 97, 102, 103, 104, 107, 108, 109, 112, 114, 118, 119, 120, 122, 124, 128, 129, 130, 133, 134, 135, 140, 142, 148, 149, 155, 161, 166, 167, 169, 171, 179, 180, 182, 190, 194, 196, 197, 198, 199, 208, 209, 210, 212, 213, 214, 220, 224, 229, 231, 235, 236, 237, 238, 244, 281, 282, 283, 284, 285, 286, 287, 289, 290, 291, 292
Franke, Hanns-Joachim: 41
Hamřík, Pavel: 29, 70
Korthaus, Edith: 252, 256, 269
Maťák, Jindřich: 233, 234, 246, 247, 248, 249, 251, 253, 277
Zahrádka, Karel: 131, 276, 280
Zukal, Rudolf: 1, 14, 30, 53, 54, 55, 72, 85, 90, 99, 101, 115, 116, 117, 123, 126, 127, 132, 136, 137, 138, 139, 141, 145, 146, 147, 150, 151, 154, 156, 157, 159, 160, 164, 165, 170, 174, 175, 177, 178, 181, 183, 184, 185, 186, 187, 189, 191, 192, 193, 195, 200, 201, 202, 203, 204, 205, 206, 207, 211, 215, 218, 219, 221, 222, 223, 226, 227, 228, 230, 232